Folens

Second Edition

Industry, Reform and Empire
Britain 1750–1900

Aaron Wilkes
James Ball

© 2008 Folens Limited, on behalf of the authors.

United Kingdom: Folens Publishers, Waterslade House, Thame Road, Haddenham, Buckinghamshire HP17 8NT.

www.folens.com

Ireland: Folens Publishers, Greenhills Road, Tallaght, Dublin 24.

Email: info@folens.ie

Editor: Daniel Bottom

Layout artist: Sally Boothroyd

Illustrations: Tony Randell and Clive Wakfer

Cover design: Mike Cryer at EMC Design

Cover image: Mary Evans Picture Library

First published 2003 by Folens Limited.

Every effort has been made to trace the copyright holders of material used in this publication. If any copyright holder has been overlooked, we should be pleased to make any necessary arrangements.

British Library Cataloguing in Publication Data. A catalogue record for this publication is available from the British Library.

ISBN 978-1-85008-346-7

Acknowledgements
Portrait of George III (1738-1820) in his Coronation Robes, c.1760 (oil on canvas), Ramsay, Allan (1713-84)/Private Collection/The Bridgeman Art Library: 6; Alamy/Allan Staley: 7 (top); The Village Fair, after 1710 (oil on copper) by Michau, Theobald (b.1676) Private Collection/Johnny Van Haeften Ltd., London/The Bridgeman Art Library: 7 (bottom); Corbis/Bettmann: 9; Museum of English Rural Life, University of Reading: 12; Getty Images/Hulton Archive: 17; Corbis/Christopher Cormack: 19; The Heart of the West Riding, 1916 by Priestman, Bertram (1868-1951) © Bradford Art Galleries and Museums, West Yorkshire, UK/The Bridgeman Art Library: 23; Mary Evans Picture Library: 27; Statens Museum for Kunst, Copenhagen: 31; Mary Evans Picture Library: 34; Christie's Images Limited: 37; Mary Evans Picture Library: 40; Science Museum/Science & Society Picture Library: 41; Mary Evans Picture Library: 44; Sheffield Galleries & Museums Trust: 48 (left); Getty Images/Mansell Collection/Time Life Pictures: 48 (right); Mary Evans Picture Library: 49; The Wellcome Trust: 52; Corbis/Hulton Archive: 53; The Wellcome Trust: 54 (left); Mary Evans Picture Library: 54 (right); Getty Images/Hulton Archive: 55 (top); Getty Images/Hulton Archive: 55 (bottom); Mary Evans Picture Library: 56; Mary Evans Picture Library: 60/61; Mary Evans Picture Library: 61 (top); Mary Evans Picture Library: 61 (bottom); Mary Evans Picture Library: 65; Art Directors & Trip Photo Library: 67; Mirrorpix: 68; Mirrorpix: 69 (top); Mirrorpix: 69 (bottom left); Getty Images/Hulton Archive: 69 (bottom right); Mary Evans Picture Library: 70; Ronald Grant Archive: 73; Mary Evans Picture Library: 75; John Bull offering Little Boney fair play, published by Hannah Humphrey in 1803 (etching) by Gillray, James (1757-1815) © Courtesy of the Warden and Scholars of New College, Oxford/The Bridgeman Art Library: 77; Imagestate/HIP/The Print Collector: 78; Getty Images/Hulton Archive: 80; Corbis/John Harper: 81 (top); Alamy/Liquid Light: 81 (bottom); Corbis/Art Archive: 82; The Duke of Wellington (after Lawrence and Evans), 1834 (w/c on paper) by Derby, William (1786-1847) © Wallace Collection, London, UK/The Bridgeman Art Library: 83 (top); Paris – Musee de l'Armee, Dist. RMN/© Pascal Segrette: 83 (bottom); The Turning Point at Waterloo (oil on canvas) by Hillingford, Robert Alexander (1825-1904): 84/85 (top); The Battle of Waterloo, 18th June 1815 (oil on canvas) by Hillingford, Robert Alexander (1825-1904) Private Collection/The Bridgeman Art Library: 84/85 (bottom); Bridgeman Art Library/Royal Holloway and Bedford New College, Surrey, UK: 87 (top); NSPCC: 87 (bottom); Mary Evans Picture Library: 88 (top); Mary Evans Picture Library: 88 (bottom); Getty Images/Hulton Archive: 88/89; Getty Images/Hulton Archive: 91; Mary Evans Picture Library: 92; Bridgeman Art Library/Royal College of Surgeons, London, UK: 94/95; Wellcome Trust Medical Photograph Library: 96; Wellcome Trust Medical Photograph Library: 97; The Mariners' Museum, Newport News, VA: 98 (top); Getty Images/Hulton Archive: 98 (bottom); Cadbury UK: 99 (top); Mary Evans Picture Library: 99 (bottom); Mary Evans Picture Library: 100 (all four); The Art Archive/Reproduced with the permission of the Trustees of Wesley's Chapel, City Road, London/John Wesley's House/Eileen Tweedy: 103; Mary Evans Picture Library: 105; Mary Evans Picture Library: 106 (top); Mary Evans Picture Library: 106 (bottom); Art Directors & Trip Photo Library: 107; Mary Evans Picture Library: 108; Mary Evans Picture Library: 109; Mary Evans Picture Library: 110 (left); Timelife Pictures/Mansell/Getty Images: 110/111; AP/PA Photos: 112 (left); Mary Evans Picture Library: 112 (right); Mary Evans Picture Library: 113 (top); Rex Features/Brandon Malone: 113 (bottom); Getty Images/Popperfoto: 114; Alamy/Colin Underhill: 115; Sotheby's Picture Library: 116; Science & Society Picture Library: 117 (top); Mary Evans Picture Library: 117 (bottom); Mary Evans Picture Library: 118; Mary Evans Picture Library: 119 (both); The Last Stand of the 24th Regiment of Foot (South Welsh Borderers) during the Zulu War, 22nd January 1879, c.1885 (oil on canvas) by Fripp, Charles Edwin (1854-1906) National Army Museum, London/The Bridgeman Art Library: 122; © Tate, London 2008: 123; Mary Evans Picture Library: 125; Bridgeman Art Library/Wilberforce House, Hull City Museums and Art Galleries, UK: 127; Mary Evans Picture Library: 128 (left); Bridgeman Art Library: 128 (right); Mary Evans Picture Library: 130; Bridgeman Art Library/Wilberforce House, Hull City Museums and Art Galleries, UK: 131 (top); Bridgeman Art Library/Wilberforce House, Hull City Museums and Art Galleries, UK: 131 (bottom); Bridgeman Art Library/British Library: 132; Western Reserve Historical Society Library, Cleveland, Ohio: 133; Corbis/Bettmann: 134; Bridgeman Art Library: 135 (both); Royal Archives, Her Majesty Queen Elizabeth II: 136; Mary Evans Picture Library: 137; Bridgeman Art Library/Courtesy of the Trustees of Sir John Soane's Museum, London: 138; Punch Limited: 140; Advertising Archive: 145.

'History Alive 3, 1789–1914', Peter Moss, Hart-Davis Education Ltd., 1984: 15, 30, 58, 59; 'Lister as I Knew Him', John Rudd Leeson, 1927, cited in 'Health and Medicine, 1750–1900', John Robottom, Longman, 1991: 96; 'Indian Home Rule', Mohandas K. Gandhi, Navajivan Publishing, 1938 (reprinted in 1946): 124; 'Pax Britannica', James Morris, 1968, cited in 'Expansion, Trade and Industry', Ros Adams, Causeway Press Ltd., 1992: 124; 'Quest: Black Peoples of the Americas', Bea Stimpson, Nelson Thornes, 2001: 129; 'The Dual Mandate in British Tropical Africa', Lord Lugard, Archon Books, 1965: 124; 'The English in India: A Problem of Politics', Sir John A. R. Marriott, Oxford University Press, 1932: 125.

Contents

What is history?

Before you start this book, take a few minutes to think about these questions.

• What do you think history is? What does the word mean?
• What have you learnt in history lessons before, perhaps in your primary school? Did you enjoy them or not? If you enjoyed them, say why. If you didn't enjoy them, why not?
• Have you read any history books or stories about things that happened a long time ago? Have you watched any television programmes, films or plays about things that happened in the past? If so, which ones?

History is about what happened in the past. It is about people in the past, what they did and why they did it, what they thought and what they felt. To enjoy history you need to have a good imagination. You need to be able to imagine what life was like in the past, or what it may have been like to be involved in past events.

How did people feel, think and react to events like these?

I am an eight-year-old child who works in a dangerous, noisy factory. I need to work to stop my family from starving. The machines have no safety guards and I have to work long hours. What will happen to me if I lose a finger or a hand... or worse?

I have just got a job on board a slave ship. Why are slaves from Africa transported to North America? How are the Africans treated? Is this trade in human beings against God's wishes?

Disease is killing hundreds of people in my street. What could be causing this disease? Is it the terrible smell? Or is it something to do with the water? What can be done to stop it?

How to use this book

As you work through this book, you will notice a number of features that keep appearing.

MISSION OBJECTIVES

All sections of this book will start by setting your Mission Objectives. These are your key aims that set out your learning targets for the work ahead. Topics will end by trying to get you to assess your own learning. If you can accomplish each Mission Objective then you are doing well!

MISSION ACCOMPLISHED?

WISE-UP Words are key terms that are vital to help you discuss and understand the topics. You can spot them easily because they are in bold type. Look up their meanings in a dictionary or use the Glossary at the end of the book. The Glossary is a list of words and their meanings.

Some topics contain PAUSE for Thought boxes. This is an opportunity for you to stop and think for yourself.

The Hungry for MORE features give you a chance to extend your knowledge and research beyond the classroom. This is a time for you to take responsibility for your own learning. You might be asked to research something in the library or on the Internet, work on a presentation, or design and make something. Can you meet the challenge?

 FACT

These are all the fascinating, amazing or astounding little bits of history that you usually don't get to hear about! But in Folens History we think they are just as important and give you insights into topics that you'll easily remember.

HISTORICAL ENQUIRY

Historical Enquiries

There are also six Historical Enquiries in this book. These will get you to focus on the following themes:

- **COULD YOU GET JUSTICE IN VICTORIAN BRITAIN?**
- **BRITAIN AT WAR**
- **HOW RELIGIOUS WAS VICTORIAN BRITAIN?**
- **BRITAIN ABROAD**
- **HOW TOLERANT WAS VICTORIAN BRITAIN?**
- **WHO RULES?**

These themes will give you a broad knowledge of medieval religion, social attitudes and rules, power and England's relations with other countries.

Work sections are your opportunity to demonstrate your knowledge and understanding. You might be asked to put events in the correct chronological order. You might be asked to:

- explain how things have changed over time;
- work out why two people might interpret the same event differently;
- work out what triggered an event to take place in the short term or the long term.

What was Britain like in 1750?

_____ MISSION OBJECTIVES _____

• To understand some of the basic details about Georgian Britain in the eighteenth century.

This book is about the people and the events of Britain between 1750 and 1900 – a time of great change. In fact, Britain probably changed more between these dates than during any other period in history. It is a time when the population grew faster than ever before and, by the end of the period, for the first time in Britain's history, more of the population lived in towns than in the countryside. It is a time when some of Britain's most famous battles took place – and when Britain gained an empire that rivalled any the world had ever seen. The period saw some of Britain's greatest inventors, politicians, medical men (and women), writers, and businessmen come to the fore. And the foundations of many of our favourite sports, high-street shops and many of our familiar customs were also laid during this period.

So how many people were there?

About 7 million people lived in Britain in 1750. However, it's hard to know the exact number because no one ever counted! Instead, historians have estimated the amount by analysing sources like church records. These list the number of baptisms and burials in any one church.

❚❚ PAUSE for Thought

Church records were not always accurate. Can you think of any reasons why they might not be? Clue: A costly registration. What problems does this cause historians?

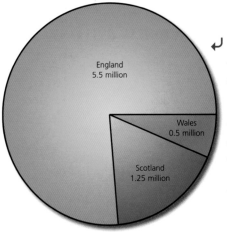

↵ SOURCE A: _A pie chart showing the estimated population in 1750. England's population was 5.5 million; Wales' 0.5 million and Scotland's 1.25 million. Ireland's population was about 3 million._

England
5.5 million

Wales
0.5 million

Scotland
1.25 million

↰ SOURCE C: _A painting of George III, King from 1760 to 1820. He was the best-known German ruler and was King for much of the period covered in this book._

SOURCE B: _In the early 1700s the writer Daniel Defoe (who wrote_ Robinson Crusoe _and the very rude_ Moll Flanders_) published a travel book called_ A Tour Through the Whole Island of Great Britain. _In this best-seller, he identified seven classes of people that he found on his journey._ ↱

Different classes found on travels:

Class 1: 'The great who live profusely'

Class 2: 'The rich who live plentifully'

Class 3: 'The middle sort, who live well'

Class 4: 'The workers, who labour hard but feel no want'

Class 5: 'The country people who manage indifferently [neither good or bad]'

Class 6: 'The poor, whose lives are hard'

Class 7: 'The miserable, who really suffer'

Who ruled?

After Queen Anne (the last of the Stuarts) died in 1714, her distant German relative, George I from Hanover, came over to rule the country. In fact, there were at least 50 other members of the royal family who had stronger claims to be the next king or queen after Anne… but they were all Catholic! Instead, German-speaking Protestant, George, took the job. The new king, mainly due to the fact that he spoke no English, left Parliament alone to rule the country – which they loved! When George I died in 1727, his son (another George) took over.

By 1750 then, George II was king – but he wasn't particularly popular because it was said that he preferred Germany! Parliament continued to make laws and hold elections every few years. The King still had to agree with all their proposals before they became law… but Parliament controlled most of the King's money, so they never had much trouble getting his support! Rich men who owned lots of land were the politicians and only other rich men could vote for them. In fact, in 1750 only 5% of men (the rich of course) could vote… and women couldn't vote at all.

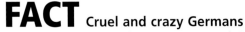

FACT Cruel and crazy Germans

From 1714 to 1820, three men named George were the kings of Great Britain and Ireland:

George I (1714–1727): Loved Germany and spent most of his time there. Famous for treating his wife very badly. He had lots of lovers but hated it when his wife Sophia Dorothea had one herself. The King ordered her lover to leave England – which he did… or so she thought! Years later, workmen found her lover's dead body under floorboards in Dorothea's bedroom!
George II (1727–1760): Son of George I. Also loved Germany and spent lots of his time there. He was the last British king to lead his army into battle against the French… again!
George III (1760–1820): Grandson of George II. People called him 'Farmer George'. Sadly, he suffered from periods of madness, during which time he ended every sentence with the word 'peacock'.

⤴ **SOURCE D:** *Downing Street was built in the 1730s and used as a home by some of the more important politicians. In 1735, George II gave house 'Number Ten' on Downing Street to Sir Robert Walpole, one of the politicians with whom he had been working closely. Other politicians teased Walpole for being so close to the King and called him 'prime minister' as an insult ('prime' means first, number one or favourite). The nickname stuck and Walpole remained Prime Minister for years to come. Ten Downing Street is still home to Britain's Prime Minister today.*

How did people have fun?

The very rich read books in the vast libraries in their country houses, took walks in their landscaped gardens, boated on their lakes or got lost in their mazes. They went hunting, fishing, to concerts, ballet shows, and played billiards and dice. Poorer people went to the local pub, where they played skittles, bowls, cards and, of course, drank beer. During holiday times they went to fairs, and gambled on bear-baiting and boxing.

↵ **SOURCE E:** *A painting of a village fair, around 1710.*

How did people die?

People didn't know that germs caused disease. Basic operations, like removing an infected toenail, could result in death because there were no painkillers or germ-free, clean, operating rooms.

The big, killer diseases were smallpox (highly infectious, causing fever, blisters, scabs… and then death!) and respiratory diseases, which affected breathing and the lungs, for example, pneumonia, bronchitis, diphtheria and tuberculosis.

The average age of death in Britain in 1750 was about 30 years of age. For every 1000 babies born, over 150 would die before they reached their first birthday… and one in five of the mothers would die too!

How did people get around?

Slowly – very slowly. There were no aeroplanes, trains or cars. Most people rarely left their village, except to go to the local town on market day. The roads were so bad that it could take up to two weeks to travel from London to Edinburgh… and four days to get from London to Exeter (and it's less than 200 miles away!). Some roads had been improved, but in 1750, they were a rare sight.

FACT Enjoy your milk

Milkmaids sold milk around the city streets in open-top buckets. One customer wrote in his diary that on its journey around the city, the milk collected 'spit, snot, dirt, rubbish, sick and lice'. Enjoy your drink!

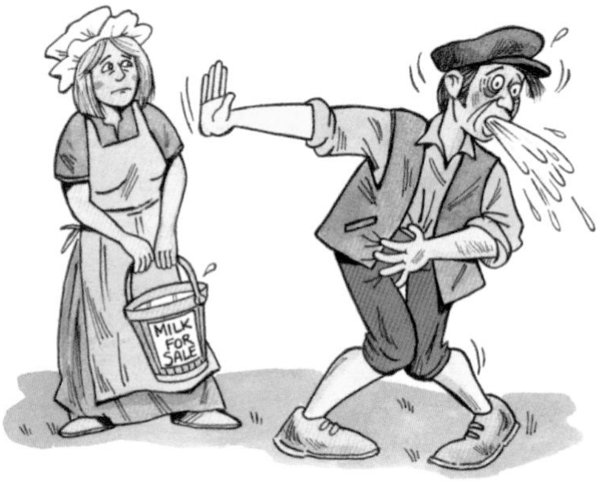
MILK FOR SALE

> 'We set out at six in the morning and didn't get out of the carriages (except when we overturned or got stuck in the mud) for 14 hours. We had nothing to eat and passed through some of the worst roads I ever saw in my life.'

SOURCE F: *Adapted from the journals of Queen Anne in 1704. They were travelling from Windsor (in Berkshire) to Petworth (in Sussex), a distance of about 40 miles.*

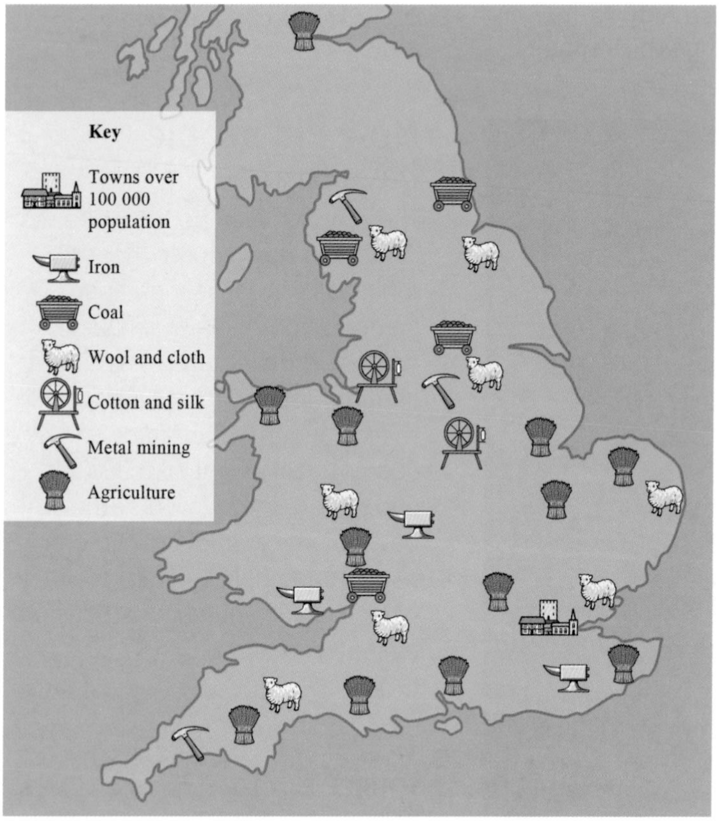
Key
Towns over 100 000 population
Iron
Coal
Wool and cloth
Cotton and silk
Metal mining
Agriculture

SOURCE G: *Major industries in 1750.*

How did people make money?

Eight out of ten people lived and worked in the countryside. They grew food and reared cattle and sheep. They grew enough to feed themselves and perhaps some extra to sell in the local town. Goods were made in people's homes or in small workshops attached to their homes. Some of the larger workshops in towns produced high-quality goods that were sold abroad. But even these businesses employed no more than 50 people. Everything a village or town needed was made by hand or on very simple machines – buttons, needles, woollen or cotton cloth, glass, bricks, pottery, candles and bread.

Some towns were growing fast (Liverpool, Leeds, Birmingham and Glasgow more than doubled in size between 1750 and 1800). Shopkeepers, chimney sweeps, flower sellers, doctors, housemaids, builders, cobblers and street traders all made a living in these fast-growing towns.

FACT Finer China

Some of the world's best-quality fine china was produced by Josiah Wedgwood, based in Stoke on Trent. His goods were sold all over the world.

How 'Great' was Britain?

By 1750, Britain was becoming a major world power.

- The British controlled areas of land in many other countries. Parts of Canada, the West Indies, Africa, India and America were under British control.

- Britain imported Indian silk, jewels, pottery, ivory, tea, American coffee, sugar, tobacco and Canadian cod. Companies sold these around Britain or they were exported to other customers abroad.

- The goods made in Britain, like cloth, pottery and iron, were sold abroad in huge numbers. All this trade made a lot of money for British companies and provided plenty of jobs for British workers.

How 'arty' was Britain?

The eighteenth century was a great age for the 'arts'. Daniel Defoe wrote *Robinson Crusoe*, Jonathan Swift wrote *Gulliver's Travels* and Samuel Johnson spent eight years writing the first ever *Dictionary of the English Language*. There were many great artists such as George Stubbs, Thomas Gainsborough and Joshua Reynolds, as well as world renowned composers, such as George Frederick Handel, who came to live in England, from Germany, in 1710.

🡅 **SOURCE H:** *Daniel Defoe's* Robinson Crusoe *is still a well-known story today.*

Work

1 **a** Write a sentence or two about the origin of the term 'Prime Minister'.

 b In 1750, who was more powerful – the King or Parliament?

 c Write a sentence or two about your Prime Minister today. Before writing your answer, you may wish to discuss the role of your Prime Minister and their powers.

2 It is 1750. Pretend you are a foreign visitor, sent on a trip to Britain by a foreign king. You must prepare a fact-file on Britain for your king back home. Use the following headings to help you:

- The people – How many? Where do they live? What do they do?

- The people in charge – Who runs the country? How? What about the royal family?

- Health of the nation – What were the common illnesses and diseases? How long could an average man expect to live?

- Travel – How advanced was Britain's transport system?

- 'Great' Britain – Were the British conquering other lands? If so, where and why?

- Leisure time – How did people have fun? How did this differ between rich and poor people?

- Culture – Who were the famous names in the fields of music, literature and painting?

Present your report as a TOP SECRET document – you never know what a foreign king might need the information for!

MISSION ACCOMPLISHED?

- Could you write out ten facts about Britain in 1750?

Why did the population 'explode'?

—— MISSION OBJECTIVES ——

- To able to explain how key factors affected the population after 1750.

Between 1750 and 1900, the population of Britain grew so fast that one historian called it 'an explosion of people'. There were about 7 million people living in Britain in 1750, with another 3 million in Ireland. By 1900, Britain's population was nearly 40 million. In other words, the population had more than quadrupled! So what was behind this 'explosion'?

There are only three possible ways for a population to increase:

i) the number of births can increase
ii) the number of deaths can decrease
iii) **immigrants** can move to the country.

Historians know that after 1750, the number of people moving to Britain was similar to the number of people leaving – so **immigration** couldn't have caused the population explosion. This leaves two other explanations.

Your task is to look through the following facts. Each has been identified by a historian as a cause of the population explosion between 1750 and 1900. Try to think whether the information in each fact would:

i) increase the number of births
ii) decrease the number of deaths
iii) do both.

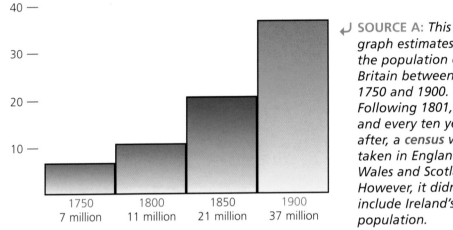

| 1750 | 1800 | 1850 | 1900 |
| 7 million | 11 million | 21 million | 37 million |

↵ SOURCE A: *This graph estimates the population of Britain between 1750 and 1900. Following 1801, and every ten years after, a census was taken in England, Wales and Scotland. However, it didn't include Ireland's population.*

Fab farmers

After 1750, farmers produced more food. People had the opportunity to enjoy a healthier diet – fresh vegetables, fruit, meat, potatoes and dairy products. All the protein and vitamins helped the body to fight disease.

Young love

After 1750, people started to get married younger. This gave couples more time to have more children.

Smelly pants

From 1800, cotton started to replace wool as Britain's most popular cloth. Cotton underwear became very popular. Cotton is much easier to wash than wool, so regular washing killed off germs.

Magic midwives

After 1750, there were improvements in the care of pregnant women by **midwives**. Some hospitals were even providing **maternity** beds by 1760.

Jenner's jabs

In 1796, Edward Jenner discovered how to vaccinate against one of Britain's worst diseases – smallpox. Gradually, more and more people were treated, until 1870, when vaccination was made compulsory for all. Smallpox disappeared.

Super soap

After 1800, cheap soap became readily available. Soap is a powerful germ-killer (although before the 1860s, people didn't know that germs caused disease).

Doctors and nurses

After 1870, doctors started to use **anaesthetics** and **antiseptics** to make operations safer and cleaner. Fewer patients died of shock, pain or infection. Nurses were better trained too. They worked in a growing number of hospitals.

Sobering up

In the 1700s, there was a craze for drinking cheap gin. Lots of **alcoholics** died as a result. Also, heavy gin drinking damaged unborn babies. In 1751, the government put a tax on gin, making it more expensive. Fewer people were able to afford it.

Cleaner cities

After the 1860s, councils began to clean up their towns and cities. Clean water supplies and sewers were installed. Better housing was built too. The healthier towns included wider, lit streets and parks for the public to use.

Baby boom

After 1800, there were more and more factories. These employed child workers. Some parents had more children knowing that they could send them out to earn money.

Clever kids

Education improved. After 1870, better schools improved **literacy**. Now people could read booklets giving advice about health, diet, cleaning, childcare and care of the sick. People began to lead healthier lives.

WISE-UP Words

alcoholic
anaesthetic   antiseptic
census   immigrants
immigration   literacy
maternity   midwives

Work

1 Write a sentence or two for each of the following words:

immigration • census • population.

2 **a** Copy Source A into your book. Remember to label it clearly.

   b Write down at least two observations about the information in the bar chart.

3 Make three lists. In one, write down all the factors that increased the number of births. In the next, write down factors that decreased the number of deaths. In the final list, write down factors that did both.

4 Use all you have learned to answer this essay question:

'Why did the population 'explode' after 1750?'

Your teacher will help you to plan it carefully. Your essay should include:
• An introduction – facts and figures about the increase in population.
• Paragraphs about the reasons for increased births and decreased deaths.
• A conclusion – a summary of your findings.

Hungry for MORE

Find out the population of Britain today. Why not create a graph or chart to represent Britain's population from 1750 to today?

MISSION ACCOMPLISHED?

• Are you able to choose any five of the key factors covered and explain how they affected the population of Britain?

What a fat pig!

- To be able to explain how farming changed and developed during the eighteenth century, and why farmers started to grow incredibly fat animals.

Take a few moments to look at Source A. It is probably one of the fattest animals you've ever seen. In fact, if a farmer today produced a pig as big as the one in the picture, he would probably be criticised for being cruel to animals! But, in the 1700s, farmers all over Britain were trying to breed larger and larger animals all the time. All over the country, pigs as fat as the one in the picture could be seen alongside huge sheep and colossal cows.

As far as the farmers were concerned, it was a case of 'bigger is better'. So why was there such a scramble to produce the fattest animals ever seen? What caused this change in breeding methods? And how else did farming change in the eighteenth century?

⤷ SOURCE A: *A pig in the late-eighteenth century.*

The old system

In the 1700s, about 80% of the population lived and worked in the countryside. Families farmed small strips of land dotted all over the village and grew enough food to feed themselves. If the harvest was especially good, they may have sold their **surplus** at market. If they owned any farm animals, these were usually allowed to roam around the common land at the edge of the village. This system had not changed very much for centuries.

But there were a number of problems with the old, established methods of farming (see Source B) and from about 1750, things began to change.

Enclosure

After 1750, the population grew rapidly. More food was needed – and the farmers had to grow it. Some farmers realised that if they had to grow more food they could make more money… but the old system of strip farming would not allow them to do this. Their answer lay in what

became known as **enclosure**. This meant a farmer buying some of their neighbour's strips of land and farming one large farm for themselves. Each owner then enclosed or surrounded their land with hedges and fences. This meant no travelling from strip to strip – and allowed individual farmers to try out new ideas and experiment with their farms in a quest to make big profits.

Any farmers left without any land (because they'd sold it) either got work on the new enclosed farms – or moved to one of the big new towns that were growing up. And any farmer who objected to enclosure could be forced to do it by Parliament if four-fifths of the village agreed to it. In fact, between 1760 and 1829, Parliament passed nearly 4000 Enclosure Acts, enclosing nearly 5 million acres of land.

Farmers wasted time travelling between their different strips, which were often hundreds of metres apart

Weeds spread easily across the strips

Fallow (unused) field had to be left for a year in order for soil to regain its nutrients

Land wasted at edge of strips where oxen turned

Land wasted between strips

The animals all mated at random, resulting in 'mongrel' cattle that were all very similar

Farmers were not free to try new ideas because everyone had to grow the same crop in the same field

Animal diseases spread easily

SOURCE B: *The problems with the old system, which was known as the 'open field system' or 'strip farming'.*

SOURCE C: *The village of Aston Blank in 1752, before and after the fields were enclosed.*

Aston Blank before enclosure

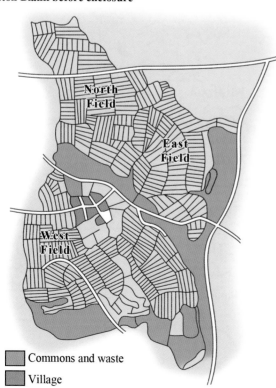

North Field

East Field

West Field

☐ Commons and waste
☐ Village

Aston Blank after enclosure

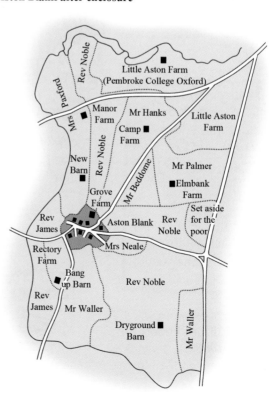

Rev Noble

Mrs Paxford

Rev Noble

Little Aston Farm (Pembroke College Oxford)

Manor Farm

Mr Hanks

Camp Farm

Little Aston Farm

New Barn

Rev Noble

Mr Beddome

Mr Palmer

Elmbank Farm

Grove Farm

Rev James

Aston Blank

Rev Noble

Set aside for the poor

Mrs Neale

Rectory Farm

Bang up Barn

Rev James

Mr Waller

Rev Noble

Dryground Barn

Mr Waller

New ideas

The big new farms allowed the best farmers to use new methods like the **four-course rotation**. This involved growing four different crops, over four years, in four different fields. One field was used for wheat (for bread), one for clover (which put nutrients into the soil), another field for growing barley or oats (for beer, food or even animal food) and the final one grew turnips or swedes (which cleaned the soil and could be used as cattle food). These crops were swapped around the fields every year. No fields were kept fallow (as under the old system) because the clover, the swedes and the turnips naturally replaced the nutrients that the wheat, barley or oats had used up… so there were bigger harvests each year. Some areas also tried **specialisation** (when a farmer concentrates on – or specialises in – growing certain crops). For example, in Kent they specialised in producing fruit and hops, while in Devon, Cider apples were the main product (see Source D).

New equipment

Some farmers experimented with bigger and better machinery, which would have been wasted on the narrow strips of the old system. For example, Jethro Tull, from Berkshire, invented a seed drill, which planted seeds in a straight row and buried them back over as protection against birds. This resulted in bigger crops and less seed being wasted.

'I conversed with several farmers. One of them said that enclosing would ruin England. It was worse than ten wars. When I asked him what he had lost by it, he replied "I kept four cows before enclosure. Now I don't keep so much as a goose. And you ask me what I lose by it!" All declared that they could see no advantage in enclosures.'

↰ SOURCE E: *Arthur Young,* Board of Agriculture Report on Bedfordshire, *1808.*

★ **WISE-UP** Words

enclosure
four-course rotation
selective breeding
specialisation
surplus

↵ SOURCE D: *Examples of specialisation.*

14

'The open field farmers had been very poor and against enclosure but are now converted. The value of sheep's wool has gone up and the price of mutton has more than doubled. There are fewer cows but the land now produces more corn and is worth more. The poor are better employed. On the whole, the measure has been beneficial.'

⌐ SOURCE F: *Arthur Young,* General View of the Agriculture of the County of Lincoln, *1813.*

New animals

Before enclosure, all of a village's animals had mixed together on the common land and bred freely. Enclosure meant that farmers could keep all their animals in separate fields – and they could control breeding to get bigger animals that would produce more meat or wool. Robert Bakewell, for example, produced big fat sheep for eating on his Leicestershire farm and the Colling brothers produced better cattle called Durham Shorthorns. Others were soon using this idea of **selective breeding** to also produce bigger pigs and better horses.

'Having found a cow with shorter legs and a thicker body than normal, the farmer would select a bull with shorter legs and a plump body and mate the two. With luck the calves would be heavier in body and shorter in leg than either parent. These calves when they grew up would be mated with other barrel-bodied beasts until heavy, meaty animals resulted. The same ideas were applied to pigs and sheep.'

⌐ SOURCE H: *An explanation of selective breeding, featured in* History Alive 3: 1789–1914 *by Peter Moss, 1984.*

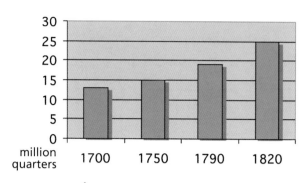

⌐ SOURCE G: *Wheat output in England and Wales (1700–1820). A quarter was about 12.72kg (nearly 13 bags of sugar).*

Work

1 Look carefully at Source B.

  a In your own words, list all the ways that land was wasted under the old, 'open-field system'.

  b Which do you think wasted the most land? Give reasons for your choice.

  c Apart from wasting valuable farmland, what other problems did farmers have when farming in this way?

2 a In your own words, explain what is meant by 'enclosure'.

  b Make a list of benefits that resulted from enclosure.

  c Can you think of some problems resulting from enclosure?

3 a Many farmers were illiterate and wouldn't have been able to read how to improve their farms with new ideas like 'four-course rotation'. Produce a poster to explain how 'four-course rotation' could help farmers improve their productivity. Limit the words on your poster as much as you can.

  b What is meant by the term 'specialisation'?

4 In your own words, explain how (and why) animals got so big after 1700. Your answer should include the phrase 'selective breeding'.

  TOP TIP: Read Source H very carefully.

1700	1800
= 370lb	= 800lb
= 28lb	= 80lb

⌐ SOURCE I: *The average weights of cattle and sheep (1700–1800).*

——**MISSION ACCOMPLISHED?**——

• Can you identify three key changes in farming during the eighteenth century and explain why each of these changes took place?

No more homework!

―――――――――――― MISSION OBJECTIVES ――――――――――――
- To be able to explain how products were manufactured in Britain in 1750.
- To understand how and why machines changed the way goods were made in Britain, forever.

In 1750, eight out of ten people lived in rural areas. Life was very tough in these places and people tried to scrape together enough food – by growing crops and keeping animals – in order to survive. But a bad harvest meant starvation for the whole family – unless they could afford to buy food from the local market. Many families protected themselves from famine by making products in their homes that they could sell for money. So what were these products? Who bought them? And why did this method of production come to an end?

It's a family affair!

The **domestic system** (domestic means involving the home or family) involved the whole household, with mums, dads and children all having their part to play. The type of goods they made depended on the area they came from but could be anything from shoes, socks, buttons, lace, hats, gloves, nails, chains or clay pots. One of the most popular goods made in people's homes was woollen cloth. This high-quality material became famous around the world and, as the population increased, was in more and more demand in Britain, too. The whole process worked like this:

'I'm freezing, he's taken all my wool.'

1 A **clothier** (wool tradesman) buys the wool from the farmer.

'I'll pick the cloth up on Thursday.'

'Slave driver!'

2 The clothier takes the wool to the villagers, who turn it into cloth.

'Our cloth is some of the best around. The clothier sells it all over Europe.'

FACT Cool cotton

It wasn't just wool that was turned into cloth. The soft fibres of the cotton plant were brought to Britain from warmer countries like India and America. The skilled British spinners would turn this into thread and then the expert weavers would weave it into a light and comfortable cloth. Cotton cloth soon became more popular than wool!

3 The family could work whatever hours they wanted... as long as they met their deadlines.

'He's getting a baa-gain!'

THURSDAY

4 The clothier returns to collect the cloth and pays the family for what they have produced. He then gives them the wool for next week's order and takes the cloth away to be dyed different colours by another family, before being sold.

! FACT Children at work

Poor children have always worked throughout history. They did jobs out on the farms like weeding and looking after animals. These jobs were boring but not particularly hard. In the factories life got much tougher!

"My job is to load, unload and carry around these heavy baskets full of equipment all day. It's exhausting!"

Some children spent years pulling and pushing heavy baskets, and their bodies became deformed as a result.

"I hardly feel like eating my breakfast because the dust, heat and smell make me feel sick."

At about 8:00am there is an half-an-hour break.

"I'm scared of Mr Willis, the overseer."

Overseers were like the factory managers and were given the job of making the children work as hard as possible. The more work the children did, the more the overseers were paid.

A common punishment in one nail-making factory in the Midlands was to hammer a nail through the offender's ear into a wooden bench.

The workers would get between 30 minutes and an hour for dinner. In some factories, the pauper apprentices didn't get any plates – instead they just held out the bottom of their shirts and the cooks poured in the food.

"Accidents are common here – none of the machines have covers or guards."

In 1833, two out of every five accident cases received at Manchester Hospital were the result of factory machinery.

On average, pauper apprentices like Peter were smaller and lighter than boys and girls of a similar age who didn't work in factories.

They generally worked a 12-hour day, but at busy times of the year it could be as long as 14 or 15 hours.

Even the children who weren't orphans and lived with their parents earned about half the amount that women did… so it was cheaper for the factory owner to employ women and children.

Goods at the owner's shop were usually of poor quality – and the workers generally rented the house from the factory owners too!

When one group got in at the end of the day, the other crawled out of the same filthy sheets of the beds that they shared.

It's work, work, work, Monday to Saturday. On Sunday we work a short day, which is four to six hours of cleaning.

The pauper apprentices were owned by the factory until they were 21. Then they often got a job in the same factory.

⤶ SOURCE A: *A drawing showing an overseer about to punish a child.*

FACT Were all bosses bad?

Some factory owners had been trying to help their workers for years. Robert Owen built quality houses, schools, shops with cheap goods for sale, galleries and parks for his workers in Scotland. He even reduced working hours. He believed that happy workers made hard workers – and he was rewarded with huge profits!

Inspector: Tell me boy, where do you live?

Child: 26 Duke Street, Leeds.

I: Do you work in the factories?

C: Yes, Sir.

I: At what age did you begin to work in them?

C: I was nearly eight years, I think.

I: How many hours a day do you work?

C: From six in the morning until seven at night.

I: Are you beaten at work?

C: Yes, Sir. If we look up from our work or speak to each other, we are beaten.

I: If you don't go as fast as the machines, are you beaten?

C: Yes, Sir. There's screaming among the boys and girls all day. They make black and blue marks on our bodies.

I: Are you allowed to 'make water' any time of the day?

C: No, only when a boy comes to tell you it's your turn. Whether you want to go or not, that's the only time you're allowed to go.

I: Can you hold your water for that long?

C: No, we're forced to let it go.

I: Do you spoil and wet yourself then?

C: Yes.

⤶ SOURCE B: *An inspector's report on children in factories. What do you think is meant by the phrase 'make water'?*

Work

1 a Write a sentence or two to explain the following words:

overseer • pauper apprentice.

2 a Make your own 24-hour timeline for a typical day in your life (choose a week day). Be careful to include:
  • all your sleep time
  • the times for eating, travelling, breaks and any spare time
  • what work you do (a paper round perhaps).

NOTE: You will also have to include something that a 14-year-old factory boy or girl wouldn't have done… school!

b Write at least five sentences, each one stating how your day is different (or similar) to a child's in 1820.

c Why do you think the treatment of children in Britain has changed so much? Explain your answer carefully – you are being asked for your opinion here.

3 Imagine you have been given the job of carrying out a factory inspection. Write a report for the government based on the information on pages 24–27.

Include sections on:
  • Dangerous and unhealthy conditions – What accidents have you heard about? Why are some children deformed? What diseases and illnesses do workers catch?

  • Cruelty and punishments – How are rule breakers treated? Are punishments appropriate?

  • The future – Why do some owners seem unwilling to make their factories safer? What improvements could be made?

You could include an interview in your report (with a factory owner and/or a worker) and a picture or diagram to illustrate your points.

—MISSION ACCOMPLISHED?—

  • Can you recall at least five facts about factory work in nineteenth-century Britain?

What was 'black gold'?

MISSION OBJECTIVES

- To understand what is meant by the term 'black gold'.
- To be able to explain why it was such a precious commodity in the 1800s.

Coal is a hard, black rock that is formed underground. Once it is lit, it burns for a long time – much longer than wood. At the start of the eighteenth century, Britain had a lot of coal in many areas. It was very cheap and was used mainly to cook with and heat houses. The workers that got the coal out of the ground – miners – didn't have to dig very deep to get at it at first. They got all they needed from large pits near the surface.

So why did the demand for coal suddenly increase? Why did coal mining turn into one of the country's most dangerous jobs? And why did some people start to refer to coal as 'black gold'?

More coal!

After 1750, more coal was needed… much, much more! There were many people with homes to heat and food to cook for a start. It was also needed to power steam engines in new factories that were springing up all over the country and was used in the making of bricks, pottery, glass, beer, sugar, soap and iron. Coal was also required to power the steam trains that travelled across the country and steam ships that sailed the seas. And the need for more coal meant more money for the mine owners. In fact, some mine owners were making so much money from their coal that they began to refer to it as 'black gold'.

Deeper and deeper

Although the demand for coal meant more money for mine owners, soon the coal near to the surface began to run out – so the miners had to dig deeper and deeper underground to get to any… and this meant DANGER!

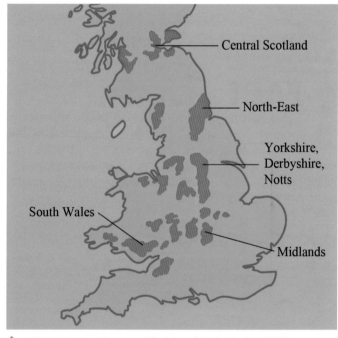

⌐ SOURCE A: *The coalfields of Britain in 1800.*

1700

1800

⌐ SOURCE B: *A diagram to demonstrate the development of mining between 1700 and 1900.*

Danny's story

As the mines got deeper, the work got harder. In fact, mining was one of the most dangerous jobs in the country. Read the following diary entry carefully. It outlines a typical day for Daniel Douglas, a 15-year-old boy in a Durham mine.

14 August 1839

What a day! I'm on the night shift this week, so I have to get to the cage at six in the evening. This mine is one of the deepest around here – 500 metres – but the drop to the bottom only takes about half a minute. The trip in the lift is dark, noisy and very scary. We drop about 30 metres every second and my eardrums always feel like they're going to burst. I hold on really tight because I don't want to fall out.

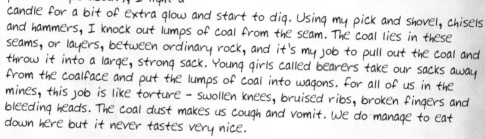

Having said goodbye to fresh air and daylight for the next ten hours, I start to 'walk out'. The four-mile walk to the coalface takes forever. By the time I actually start working, I've been down the pit for over an hour!

After hanging up my safety lamp (it burns brighter if there's any poisonous gas about), I light a candle for a bit of extra glow and start to dig. Using my pick and shovel, chisels and hammers, I knock out lumps of coal from the seam. The coal lies in these seams, or layers, between ordinary rock, and it's my job to pull out the coal and throw it into a large, strong sack. Young girls called bearers take our sacks away from the coalface and put the lumps of coal into wagons. For all of us in the mines, this job is like torture – swollen knees, bruised ribs, broken fingers and bleeding heads. The coal dust makes us cough and vomit. We do manage to eat down here but it never tastes very nice.

The only things that ever make us smile are the canaries, chirping away in their cages. We just keep our fingers crossed that they don't stop singing! We don't like to talk about accidents... but we all know people who've been killed down here. Floods, roof-falls, explosions and poisonous gas claim the lives of dozens every year.

After eight hours of hot, dirty work on my knees, it's time to make my way back up to the surface. I always have a chat with some of the trappers on my way out because it was the job I used to do when I first started working here ten years ago. Those little children open and close trapdoors to let the coal wagons pass by on the underground tracks. Drawers push and pull the loaded wagons towards the lifts that take them up to the surface.

When they're not taking any coal up, the lifts take us back up to the surface – about 11 hours after I first started! Like I said, I'm working the night shift this week so it's daylight when I finish work. The mine never closes – 24 hours a day it runs – and it must be making the owner a fortune. No wonder they've started to call coal 'black gold'.

Before I collapse into bed, I check on my pigeons (I race them, you see), have a cup of tea and a bite to eat before falling into a very deep sleep. I'll be back at the lift later this evening when it all starts over again.

Accident

As you will have worked out, working down a mine could be a very risky business. The hours were long, the pay was low (although better than in some factories) and the conditions were very, very harsh. Most mine owners thought only about making as much money as possible, so they rarely spent any money on safety measures. There were many terrible accidents and it is little wonder that miners had a lower life expectancy than most other workers!

Illness

Accidents didn't always kill but losing fingers, hands or feet in rock falls was common and miners often suffered from a variety of illnesses.

There were over 1000 deaths down the mines every year. It was such a dangerous job that in Scotland, some criminals who were sentenced to death were offered the choice of execution... or working down the coal mines!

Causes of Death	Age		
	Under 13	13–18	18+
Gas explosion	12	21	43
Gunpowder explosion	1	0	1
Crushed	0	0	3
Suffocated (by choke damp)	3	0	8
Drowned	8	3	9
Hit by falling coal, stones and rubbish	23	20	55
Fall from the shafts	7	15	35
Fall from the rope breaking	0	2	3
Fall when ascending	2	2	6
Hit by wagons	5	3	9
Drawn over the pulley	5	2	3
Injuries in coal mines (unspecified)	10	6	25
Total	**76**	**74**	**200**

⤴ **SOURCE B:** *Causes of death in a Yorkshire mine, 1805.*

Arthritis and **rheumatism** caused painful swelling and stiffness in muscles and joints, and was caused by years of crawling around on knees and elbows in damp conditions.

'Black lung' was the nickname given to severe coughing fits. Years and years of fine, black dust would collect in a miner's lungs, leaving him short of breath and constantly coughing up black mucus.

Nystagmus was an eye illness caused by years of straining to see in poor light. It made miners' eyes very sore and they would find it difficult to focus.

'Because of the water, the filth and the heat, men, women and children often worked stark naked in the slushy, black mud in the dark tunnels. It is little wonder that they lived like animals below ground, and often little better when they reached the surface ... working 12 or more hours under the ground, and going down before dawn and coming up after dark, many saw daylight only on Sunday.'

⤴ SOURCE C: *A modern historian, Peter Moss, describes a miner's life,* History Alive 3, 1789–1914.

Time for a change?

Despite these facts, the coal mines continued to make lots and lots of money for their owners as they produced more and more coal. Eventually though, the government started to take notice of all the accidents. A report on conditions in the mines was published in 1842 and the information, interviews and pictures shocked the nation. The mine owners didn't want the government to interfere with the way they ran their mines as they feared this might affect their profits. However, the evidence from the 1842 *Mines Report* was overwhelming – perhaps the government would soon start to pass laws to protect the miners!

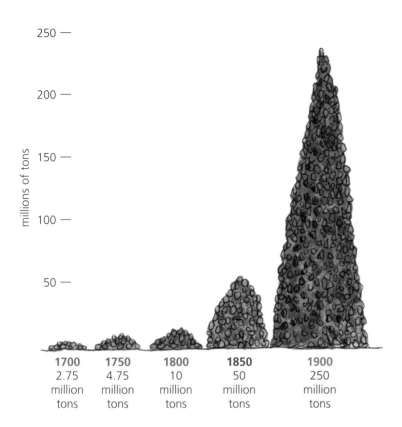

millions of tons

250 —

200 —

150 —

100 —

50 —

1700	1750	1800	1850	1900
2.75 million tons	4.75 million tons	10 million tons	50 million tons	250 million tons

↥ SOURCE D: *Coal production (1700–1900).*

↥ SOURCE E: *A painting called* The Wounded Workman. *Can you see:*
i) his tearful wife?
ii) the grave crosses of dead workers?

WISE-UP Words

arthritis   bearers
black lung   coalface
drawers   miners   nystagmus
rheumatism   trappers

Work

1 a After 1750, why were deeper mines needed?

b List all the dangers involved in mining. You should be able to find at least eight on pages 28–31.

c Look at Source E. Write down at least three words or phrases to describe this famous painting. Explain why you have chosen these words.

2 Read Daniel Douglas' diary entry carefully.

a At what age did he begin working down the mine?

b Explain carefully what Daniel used to do when he first started to work in the mine.

c What did 'bearers' and 'drawers' do?

d Why might Daniel be able to see daylight when he was trying to get to sleep after work?

e According to Daniel, why is the mine owner making so much money?

3 a Why do you think the *Mines Report* of 1842 shocked the nation?

b Why do you think some mine owners didn't want the government to interfere in their business? Explain your answer carefully.

c Imagine you are a Member of Parliament in 1842. You are part of the investigation team who wrote the *Mines Report*. You want to get some changes introduced and decide to hold a public meeting to gain support.

i) Design a poster to advertise the meeting.

ii) Write out a brief speech that you could make.

—MISSION ACCOMPLISHED?—

• Can you explain how and why coal mining changed after 1750?

• Can you explain why many people used the term 'black gold' to describe coal?

A new 'Age of iron'

MISSION OBJECTIVES

- To explain how iron was produced and how this process was improved.
- To know which family made advances in iron production.
- To understand how important iron was for the Industrial Revolution.

The eighteenth century saw major advances in the use and production of iron. It had been produced in Britain since Roman times but in the 1700s it began to be used in all areas of life. The army used it for cannons, the navy for 'iron-clad' ships, and the new factories were held up with iron girders and used iron machines that were powered by iron steam engines! It was used for tools, trains and their tracks, and at home people sat around fireplaces with iron grates and cooked on iron stoves using iron pans. So how was iron made? How was this process improved? And who went 'iron mad' in this new 'Age of iron'?

1 Iron ore is dug from the ground.

2 The ore is then melted together with limestone (to remove impurities) and charcoal (baked wood) in a furnace. Huge bellows 'blast' air in to raise the temperature. Hot liquid iron separates from the ore and pours out.

3 Red hot, liquid iron is then poured into casts shaped like pots, pans, pipes, cannons, beams and so on. **Cast iron** is strong but contains air bubbles that can make it brittle.

4 When cast iron is reheated and hammered, the pockets of air are removed and it becomes **wrought iron**. This is purer, stronger, more bendy and is used for chains, tools, furniture, train tracks and so on.

⤵ SOURCE A: *How to make iron in the 1700s.*

The kings of Coalbrookdale!

As the population and the number of factories grew, so did the demand for iron. But the producers of iron faced a problem – Britain was running out of forests! Charcoal was needed in order to **smelt** the iron ore, as coal contained too much sulphur and produced poor quality iron. Luckily for Britain, a family called the Darbys became involved in the iron industry.

> In 1709 I discovered a way of using coal to smelt iron! All you need to do is heat it first in order to remove the sulphur and create coke. Cast iron made with coke is much better quality than cast iron made with coal – iron production could continue!

Abraham Darby I 1678–1717

> I improved the process invented by father, removing even more impurities and allowing wrought iron to be made from coke-fired coal!

Abraham Darby II 1711–1763

Abraham Darby III 1750–1791

> I carried on the good work of my father and grandfather and decided to show what is possible using their iron with this magnificent iron bridge! Now our ironworks at Coalbrookdale is famous throughout the world!

Ironbridge – one of the wonders of the world!

The iron bridge over the River Severn at Coalbrookdale, Shropshire, was a massive success. When it opened on New Year's Day 1781, it caused a sensation. Writers, artists and rich tourists came from all over the world to see this modern miracle – and Darby charged every one of them to walk across it! It was also a fantastic advertisement for just what could be achieved with iron and iron production became one of Britain's most important industries (see Source B). No wonder people began to call the period: the 'Age of iron'.

Year	How much was produced in Britain?
1750	30 000 tons
1800	250 000 tons
1850	2 000 000 tons
1900	6 000 000 tons

SOURCE B: *Iron produced in Britain 1750–1900. After 1856, steel (made from iron) started to be produced in Britain, too.*

! FACT Iron mad!
It wasn't just the Darbys who were obsessed with finding new uses for iron. John 'iron mad' Wilkinson built an iron barge in 1787 and, later, built an iron church for his workers. When he died, he was even buried in an iron coffin under an iron headstone!

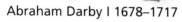

WISE-UP Words

cast iron
coke
ironworks
smelt
wrought iron

Work

1 Using no more than three sentences, explain how iron is produced.

2 Explain the difference between cast iron and wrought iron.

3 Explain why Abraham Darby I was so important in increasing Britain's iron production?

4 Copy and complete the following paragraph:

The most famous iron makers of them all were the _____ family from _____, Shropshire. Their _____ was one of the finest in the world. One member of the family was so keen to show his iron off, he built the world's first _____ _____ over the River _____.

5 Look at Source B. Draw a bar graph to show how Britain's iron production increased.

6 List three iron items that were essential for Britain's industry to become mechanised.

MISSION ACCOMPLISHED?

• Could you tell someone how cast and wrought iron were produced?

• Do you know which family improved iron production?

• Could you name three things that were made out of iron?

The end of the 'cripple factory'

MISSION OBJECTIVES
- To identify why some factory owners were unwilling to improve working conditions.
- To be able to recall three key reforms that eventually improved life for Britain's workers.

In 1800, a factory in Manchester was given a terrifying nickname. It was known as the 'Cripple Factory'. Years and years of heavy lifting, broken arms and severe beatings meant that many of the young men, women and children who worked there were crippled forever. The mines weren't much better either. One 11-year-old girl working as a coal-carrier describes her job in Source A. Source B also gives an idea of what her job entailed.

Today, the government would not let this sort of thing happen. Many people in 1800 thought that politicians had no right to interfere with the working conditions in factories. They believed that it was up to the owners to decide how they ran their factories and mines. After all, they owned them, didn't they? Many felt the government had no right to meddle in the private arrangement between a worker and an employer. This attitude was called *laissez-faire*, French words meaning 'leave alone'.

Some argued that people might work harder if they were treated better! **Reformers** like Lord Shaftesbury, Richard Oastler, John Fielden and Michael Sadler (another MP) began to campaign for laws to protect factory and mine workers. Protection of the children was seen as the first priority, then women and later the men.

'I go down the pit at two in the morning and I don't come up again until the next afternoon. I go to bed at six at night to be ready for work the next morning... I carry coal tubs up ladders all day. Each coal tub holds 41/4 cwt* [216 kilos – about as heavy as three adults] and I get beaten when I don't work hard enough.'

↱ SOURCE A: *Working in a mine. (*cwt = hundredweight)*

Some men collected evidence to prove how bad things were. Their findings shocked the nation.

Interviewer: Were you sometimes late?
Matthew: Yes, and if we were even five minutes late, we were beaten black and blue by the overseer. He hit us with a strap.
Interviewer: Do you know of any accidents?
Matthew: Yes, there was a boy who got hit by a machine. He broke both legs and one of them was cut open from his knee to his waist. His head was cut, his eyes were nearly torn out and he broke both arms.
WARNING! This interview is taken from a report by an MP called Michael Sadler. Some historians think he exaggerated the answers when writing up his investigation. He wanted conditions to appear even worse than they already were. Regardless of this, the Sadler Report made a huge impact.

↱ SOURCE C: *A few questions and answers from the* Sadler Report, *an investigation into factory conditions in 1832. Dozens of workers like Matthew Crabtree were interviewed.*

SOURCE B: *Tough work in the mining industry.* ↴

> 'I have a belt around my waist and I go on my hands and feet... the belt and chain are worse when we are in the family way [pregnant]. I've had three or four children born on the same days as I have been at work and have gone back to work nine or ten days later. Four out of my eight children were still-born.'

↳ **SOURCE D:** *From the* Mines Report *of 1842. Betty Harris, aged 37, describes her work. She pulled coal along in large wagons.*

After reading the reports, Parliament acted. From 1833, new laws or Acts made great changes to the working lives of women and children. Men, it was believed, could look after themselves.

Some factory owners hated the changes. They felt politicians had no right to interfere in their business and thought of ways to avoid keeping to the new rules. But the new laws kept coming and, gradually, they began to protect more and more workers. Inspectors were even appointed to enforce them!

By 1900, factories and mines had become safer and more bearable. They still weren't particularly pleasant places to work but Parliament had accepted that they had a duty to look after the more vulnerable people in society.

1833 FACTORY ACT
- No children under nine to work in the factories.
- Nine hours work per day for children aged 9–13.
- Two hours school per day.
- Factory inspectors appointed (but there were only four!).

1842 MINES ACT
- No women or children under ten to work down a mine.
- Mine inspectors appointed.

1844 FACTORY ACT
- No women to work more than 12 hours per day.
- Machines to be made safer.

1847 TEN HOUR ACT
- Maximum ten-hour day for all women and workers under 18.

1850 FACTORY ACT
- Machines to only operate between 6:00am and 6:00pm.

1871 TRADE UNION ACT
- Trade unions made legal. Workers all doing the same job (trade) – like railway workers or dockers, for example – were allowed to join together (union) to negotiate with their employers for improvements to pay and working conditions. As a last resort, all union members could go on strike!

1895 FACTORY ACT
- Children under 13 to work a maximum of 30 hours per week.

↳ **SOURCE E:** *New acts to protect workers.*

WISE-UP Words

laissez-faire
reformer

Work

1 a How did the 'Cripple Factory' get its terrifying nickname?

b In your opinion, were the mines just as bad as some factories? Support your answer using evidence from some of the sources.

2 a Explain what is meant by the term '*laissez-faire*'.

b Why did some factory owners believe in '*laissez-faire*'?

c Explain the word 'reformer'.

d How did reformers bring about changes to working conditions?

e Did all factories need reforming? Explain your answer carefully.

3 Look at Source C.

a Write down three of the most important changes to working conditions between 1830 and 1895.

b Next to each one, explain why you think it was an important change.

4 Look at Source D.

a Write down three words or phrases that a reader of this report might feel.

b Why might this interview NOT be totally reliable? Give reasons for your answer.

c Do any of Matthew's answers seem a bit exaggerated? Explain your answer.

d How could a historian get a more reliable view of factory life in the 1800s? You might want to discuss this question with your classmates or teacher.

—MISSION ACCOMPLISHED?—

- Can you recall three key industrial reforms and explain how they improved working conditions?

Turnpike fever!

MISSION OBJECTIVES

- To be aware of the problems with Britain's transport system in 1750.
- To understand how the roads were improved.

Take two of Britain's most important cities: London and Edinburgh. The distance between them is about 420 miles but if you travelled from one city to the other in 1750, it would have taken you a week by boat and two weeks by road. That's right – two whole weeks of travelling to get there! By 1900, you could make the same journey in just nine hours! How was this improvement possible? And just how was time spent travelling reduced by so much?

Hit the road, Jack!

In 1750, Britain's roads were in a sorry state. They always had been but they were now busier than ever. Coal had to be taken from the mines to the factories and then to the towns, in order to heat people's homes. Cotton also had to be moved from the ports to the factories before the finished goods had to be moved to market. A fast and reliable postal service was needed for businessmen too. Many people used the sea or rivers to get around – especially when moving heavy goods like iron or coal – but dozens of towns were miles from the nearest river. For them, the only alternative was to take to the road – and they met a host of problems!

Stand and deliver!

Britain's roads were lonely, isolated places that were completely unlit at night. As soon as travellers left the safety of the towns, they were sitting targets for highwaymen. With no hope of sending for help, passengers in a **stagecoach** often found themselves handing over valuables while looking down the barrel of a gun!

The rocky road to ruin

Even if you weren't the victim of an armed robbery, Britain's roads were still dangerous places. They were so rutted and full of huge potholes that coaches often became stuck or had their wheels smashed. Some of the potholes were so big that people actually drowned in them! Every villager was supposed to spend six days each year repairing the roads. But as they only rarely left their fields, the roads got worse and worse the further you got away from the village.

'Let me warn all travellers... to avoid this road like the Devil. They will meet here with ruts, which actually measured four feet deep and floating with mud in the summer. What can it be like in winter? I passed three carts broken down in 18 miles.'

↰ **SOURCE A:** *Written by Arthur Young, a traveller.*

36

WISE-UP Words

stagecoach
toll
toll keepers
turnpike trust

Time for the turnpikes!

The government could see businesses were losing money because of the terrible roads and decided to act. They divided Britain's main roads up and rented each section to a '**turnpike trust**'. These trusts promised to improve their few kilometres of road and keep it in good order. In return, the trusts were allowed to charge a **toll** from every person that used their section of road. Turnpike roads, as they became known, had gates at the end of each stretch of road where **toll keepers** collected the money. Much of the cash collected was used to improve the roads and specialist engineers went on to create the finest roads Britain had ever seen.

By 1830, there were nearly 1000 turnpike trusts improving over 20 000 miles of British roads. The effect they had was dramatic. It might have taken you two weeks to travel from London to Edinburgh in 1750 – but by 1830 you could make the same journey in about 48 hours!

Work

1 a How long did it take to get from London to Edinburgh by road in 1750?

b Why do you think the journey took so long? Use Sources A and B to explain your answer.

c Why didn't more people use water transport instead of the roads?

2 a Match up the names on the left with the correct descriptions on the right:

turnpike trust — a small fee or tax paid for using the road

turnpike road — a group of businessmen, responsible for improving a stretch of road and keeping it in good order

toll — the person who collects the tolls at the beginning of the journey

toll keeper — a road controlled by a turnpike trust.

b Read this list of people:

farmers • factory owners • businessmen • the army • horse and coach companies • the Post Office.

Decide which groups gained by having better roads. In each case, give reasons why they benefited.

3 a Copy Source C into your book.

b In what ways are these roads better than the road described in Source A?

c By 1830, how long did it take to get from London to Edinburgh?

A Telford Road

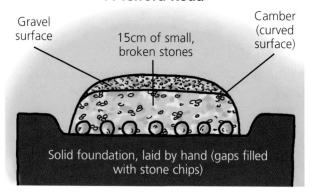

Gravel surface

15cm of small, broken stones

Camber (curved surface)

Solid foundation, laid by hand (gaps filled with stone chips)

A McAdam Road

15cm of granite chippings

Camber

Road raised above ground level

Two layers of small, rough stones at bottom

↵ **SOURCE C:** *Thomas Telford and John McAdam were Britain's most famous road builders. McAdam's roads were most popular – they were cheaper – and hundreds of trusts paid for 'McAdamised' roads. Years later, tar was added to the surface and it became known as 'tarmac'.*

—MISSION ACCOMPLISHED?—

• Could you describe two problems that travellers faced on Britain's roads in 1750?

• Could you tell someone how turnpikes improved Britain's roads?

• Do you know how long it took to travel from London to Edinburgh by road in 1830?

Canal mania!

—————————— MISSION OBJECTIVES ——————————
- To explain why even turnpike roads weren't suitable for some businessmen.
- To be able to define what a canal is and know why the Duke of Bridgewater built one.
- To know the reasons why 'canal mania' ended.

The turnpikes had given Britain some of the best roads in the world and journey times had been made much shorter – but many businessmen still weren't happy. They were convinced that their profits could be increased if a different form of transport was used. So what were the problems with the new roads? What solution did they come up with? And was this the answer to Britain's transport problems?

Warning! Wide load!

The growth of towns and increase in factories meant that the roads were busier than ever. But it wasn't just the amount of vehicles on the roads that caused businessmen headaches – it was the kind of things they were carrying. Factories powered by steam engines needed a constant supply of coal and the new ironworks were delivering huge, heavy objects all over the country. This was a lot for a poor horse to drag – especially uphill!

Bridgewater's brains!

The Duke of Bridgewater owned coal mines in Worsley. Although there was a great demand for his coal just nine miles away in Manchester, he couldn't get it there quick enough. It was also costing him a fortune in tolls as the horses and carts had to pay every time they made the journey. Bridgewater realised that if he built an inland waterway between Manchester and his mines, not only would he avoid the tolls, he could move – and sell – a whole lot more coal! He borrowed a fortune and turned to a brilliant engineer called James Brindley to cut him Britain's first industrial **canal**.

Brilliant Brindley!

A canal is a long, narrow, man-made channel of still water – a bit like a giant bath! It has to remain completely level all the way along or the water would flow downhill and empty the canal. Unfortunately for Bridgewater, the River Irwell and its steep valley ran right across the path of his canal. He had to think of a way of getting boats across this valley – and his solution was Britain's first **aqueduct**. This basically carried the canal over the valley on legs and was described as the 'most extraordinary thing in the Kingdom, if not in Europe'.

What a smashing idea!

Another businessman, Josiah Wedgwood, decided he wanted a canal for different reasons. Wedgwood had cashed in on the popularity of drinking tea and had a thriving business making thousands of cups, saucers and teapots at his pottery in Stoke. Yet he was not making as much money as he could have because some of his goods were being smashed on their bumpy journey to the market. Canal barges guaranteed a much smoother ride than any road and more of Wedgwood's delicate china was soon reaching his customers in one piece.

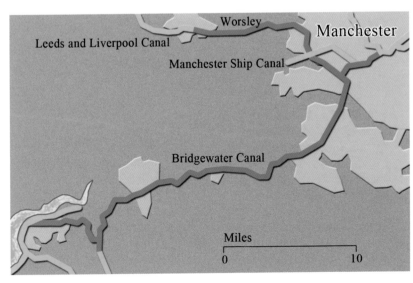

↵ **SOURCE A:** *The Bridgewater Canal opened on 17 July 1761 and was an instant success. It might have cost a fortune to build but the Duke's coal got to Manchester twice as fast and for half the price of road travel!*

Canal crazy!

As inland water ways were ideal for moving heavy, bulky goods like coal and iron, and perfect for moving fragile, breakable goods like pottery, they soon caught on. By 1830, 4000 miles of canal had been built and it was possible to travel to every major town and city in England by barge. 'Canal mania' provided work for thousands of **navvies** (as the men who built them were known) as they all had to be dug out by hand.

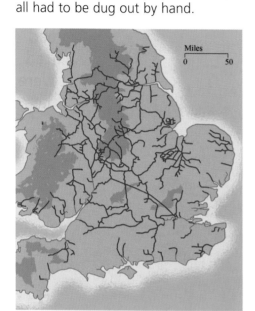

⌐ SOURCE B: *Soon, every town in England could be reached by canal.*

Locked up!

Not every canal builder used aqueducts to get up and down hills – many decided to use canal locks. These are gated boxes that help to control the water level of the canal by allowing (or not allowing) different amounts of water to pass through. It wasn't as quick as an aqueduct or tunnel but it was cheaper to build and did get the job done!

The great age of canal building did not last long. They were too slow to transport mail (fast mail coaches could carry light items quicker), they could freeze up in winter and dry out in summer. There wasn't really any passenger service on the canals either but, by the 1830s, inventors had come up with a new form of transport. Britain was entering the age of the train!

WISE-UP Words

aqueduct
canal   navvies

Work

1 Use all the information on these two pages:

  a Make a list of all the reasons why roads were not suitable for some people.

  b Make another list of reasons why canals were useful to Bridgewater, Wedgwood and other businessmen.

  c Make a final list which shows some of the problems associated with canals.

2 What do you think the phrase 'canal mania' means? Explain your answer fully.

3 a Draw this puzzle in your book and fill in the answers to the clues:

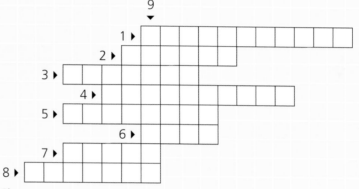

Clues:

  1 It was his idea
  2 The canal needed to go over this river
  3 Men employed to build the canals
  4 Coal was needed here
  5 This carried the canal over the river
  6 A way of allowing a canal to go up and down hills
  7 Wedgwood made pottery here
  8 Where the coal mines were

  b Read 9 down in the puzzle. Write a sentence about this person.

↵ SOURCE C: *Locks allowed barges to move up and downhill.*

___ **MISSION ACCOMPLISHED?** ___

• Do you know why roads were no good for the Duke of Bridgewater?

• Can you explain why Josiah Wedgwood built a canal?

• Could you tell someone the limitations of canals?

Iron horses

──────────────MISSION OBJECTIVES──────────────
- To be able to define what the word 'locomotive' means.
- To be able to explain why the Liverpool and Manchester Railway Company was so important and who won the Rainhill Trials competition.

By 1820, there were 1500 miles of railway track in Britain. All the tracks were quite short – going from mines to canals – and horses were mostly used to drag the wagons. But in 1826 all that changed when the Liverpool and Manchester Railway Company was formed. It didn't plan to use horses to pull carriages along the track… it was going to use locomotives! So what is a locomotive? What else was different about this railway? And why did 'iron horses' replace real ones?

Do the locomotion!

As soon as James Watt and Matthew Boulton built a steam engine that could turn a wheel, it was just a question of time before a **locomotive** was made. A locomotive is an engine that moves along rails and the man credited with building the first one was Richard Trevithick. In 1804, his engine pulled ten tons of iron and 70 passengers for nine miles – but it took four hours! It would have been quicker to walk but this new 'iron horse', as they were called, could pull far heavier loads than actual horses. Other mine owners soon copied the idea and, by 1825, several railways were using both horse AND locomotive-drawn wagons on their tracks. The Stockton to Darlington railway even pulled passenger carriages and was the world's first public transport system to use a locomotive. But, in 1829, the next big breakthrough came – and Britain would never be the same again.

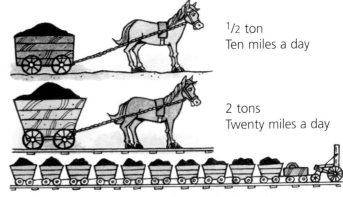

½ ton
Ten miles a day

2 tons
Twenty miles a day

40 tons   Two hundred miles a day

↰ **SOURCE A:** *Transport of goods by road and rail.*

A tale of two cities

A group of businessmen in the north-west of England saw the opportunity of making a fortune by linking two major cities. By building a railway between Liverpool and Manchester, businesses in both cities could trade large amounts of goods quickly and easily – and the railway company would charge them every time they did! They hired a man called George Stephenson – who had built several railways for pit owners – to lay the 30 miles of track between Liverpool and Manchester. It was no easy task and required the building of 63 bridges, a **viaduct** that carried the tracks over a river and a huge tunnel. By 1829, Stephenson had conquered the engineering problems and the railway was complete. Now all that was needed was a fast and reliable locomotive.

↵ **SOURCE B:** *The railway also had to pass through a huge bog called Chat Moss. Stephenson moved thousands of tons of stone in order to stop the trains sinking in the marsh!*

Stitched up!

In 1865, the Singer 'New family sewing machine' went on sale. This meant that people could make and repair their own clothes cheaply and easily and, within 20 years, over 4 million Singer's had been sold!

Baby you can drive my car !

The first car with a petrol engine was invented by a Belgian man called Lenoir in 1863 and later improved by two Germans called Karl Benz and Gottlieb Daimler. They weren't very fast – especially in Britain, where the Red Flag Act set the speed limit at 4mph! The same law also said that cars had to have someone walking in front of them waving a red flag to warn people that it was coming!

You've been framed!

English man William Henry Fox Talbot had a problem – he couldn't draw! So he decided to invent a machine that used lenses and light-sensitive paper to make the sketches for him. In 1835, he made the world's first negative and then printed photographs from it. This meant that life-like portraits of people could be made quickly and cheaply and soon most people had a mantlepiece crowded with photos. It also meant that, for the first time, people could see exactly what Royals and other famous people actually looked like. Collecting their pictures became a popular hobby and the obsession with celebrities began!

Thank you for the music!

In 1877, an American named Thomas Edison invented a machine that he called the phonograph. It was able to record sounds and then play them back and caused an international sensation! It worked by scratching a needle over a tin-foil drum but the drums could only be used once before they had to be thrown away. In 1887, Emile Berliner started to use vinyl disks, or 'records', instead of drums on his 'gramophone'. Not only could the vinyl disks be played hundreds of times but endless copies could be mass-produced from master disks. Soon, people were collecting and listening to records of all the music stars – and have been ever since.

Ice! Ice! Baby!

People had always known that cold temperatures made food last longer and big mansions often had ice houses (underground rooms packed with winter ice) in which meat was kept. In 1748, scientists at the University of Glasgow worked out a way of cooling air by quickly vaporising gases. Refrigerators slowly developed but the poisonous gases that were used did put some people off using them. In 1880, the first cargo of frozen meat arrived from Australia and soon Argentina was supplying Britain with cheap meat. This greatly improved the diets of poor people but put many British farmers out of business.

WISE-UP Words

labour saving

Work

1 Explain what the term 'labour saving' means.

2 **a** Place the machines in what you think is the order of their importance – but write them in your exercise books using Morse code!

b Write a paragraph explaining why you have put them in the order you have.

3 Make a list of labour-saving devices that you use regularly. Choose just one, that you couldn't live without.

OK computer!

Believe it or not, the computer can be traced back to Queen Victoria's reign. In 1849, an Englishman named Charles Babbage designed his 'Difference Engine', which could compute complicated mathematical tables. But it wasn't like any computer you might use today as there was no keyboard, screen or even electrical power! It was operated by cranking a handle which turned hundreds of cogs and printed out the results of the computation. Babbage never built his machine but, in 1991, the London Science Museum made one using the original plans. It worked perfectly!

—MISSION ACCOMPLISHED?—

- Could you tell someone about three inventions from the Victorian era that we still use today?
- Have you decided which was the most important and explained why?

So what was the Industrial Revolution and why did it happen?

_____ MISSION OBJECTIVES _____

• To analyse and understand the causes of the Industrial Revolution?

Historians like to give labels to different periods of time – the 'Ice Age', the 'Stone Age', the 'Norman Conquest', the 'Middle Ages' and the 'Tudor Period' are all good examples. The period of time covered in this book, 1750 to 1900, also has a label. These two pages aim to discover how it got its name… and what caused this 'Industrial Revolution' to happen.

It was a British writer, Arnold Toynbee (1852–1883), who first used the label 'Industrial Revolution'. He was using it to describe the huge changes that had occurred in the way people worked in the years after 1750. This was the time when the **manufacturing** of all kinds of goods moved out of people's homes and into the new steam-powered factories. Dozens of clever, new machines made all sorts of goods in a fraction of the time it would have taken someone to make in their own home. By 1830, one operator working several factory machines could produce three-and-a-half thousand times more cloth than a person working at home could have done in 1700! It is easy to see why Toynbee used his label – 'industrial' is another word for 'work' and 'revolution' is an alternative word for 'change'. Certainly then, between 1750 and 1900, industry in Britain had undergone a massive revolution.

As the years have passed, the label 'Industrial Revolution' has not just meant changes associated with the way people worked. It is now used to describe the changes that took place in the period of time as a whole – changes in the population, transport, towns and cities, medicine, science and technology, and so on. Today, these changes are said to have happened 'during the Industrial Revolution'. So why did the Industrial Revolution take place?

Most historians agree that there weren't just one or two things that caused the Industrial Revolution to start. Instead, there was a combination of five or six factors that all came together in the same country at a similar time.

There were more people

Between 1750 and 1900, the population increased – massively.

All these people needed shirts, trousers, coats, socks, shoes, plates, knives, forks, clocks and so on. The factories that produced these goods made a fortune for their owners – and there was plenty of work to go around too! Britain changed as factories were built to provide work for the growing population... and made lots of goods for them to buy.

Britain gained an empire

During this time, Britain gained a huge Empire. At one point, Britain ruled about 450 million people living in 56 colonies all over the world. Britain ruled huge countries like Canada, India, Australia – and most of North America – up to 1783. Britain's was the biggest Empire the world had ever known! These colonies bought British-made goods of all kinds, especially cloth, iron and later steel. British traders were happy to sell as much as they could.

INDIAN COTTON

Britain changed as its Empire grew. Cheap goods, like cotton, were imported from the colonies; the factories turned it into cloth... and sold some of it back for huge profits!

There were some clever entrepreneurs

Entrepreneurs are business people who are prepared to take risks. They buy **raw materials** (like clay), make it into goods (like teapots) and sell the goods for a profit. Between 1750 and 1900, there were large numbers of risk-taking entrepreneurs. Banks were willing to lend them money to put into new businesses, factories and inventions if they looked like they would give them a profit.

There were many brilliant inventors

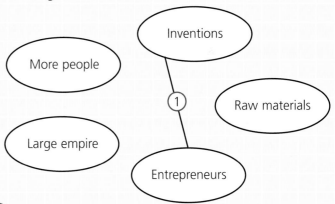

Between 1750 and 1900, some of the world's greatest inventors happened to live in Britain. Clever inventors thought up wonderful machines that produced more food, more cloth and more iron faster than ever before. Steam engines, steam trains, electric generators, telephones and light bulbs are just a few 'British firsts'. Britain changed as it became a world leader in technology.

Britain had lots of coal and iron

Britain was blessed with some valuable raw materials. By 1850, Britain produced two-thirds of the world's coal, half of the world's iron, two-thirds of the world's steel and half of the world's cotton cloth! No wonder Britain was sometimes called the 'workshop of the world'. Others just called it 'Great Britain'.

WISE-UP Words

Industrial Revolution
manufacture
raw materials

Work

1 In your own words, explain what the label 'Industrial Revolution' actually means.

2 All the following factors were important in creating an 'Industrial Revolution' in Britain. Your task is to show how these factors worked together to bring about the Industrial Revolution:

```
        Inventions

More people
                    (1)    Raw materials

Large empire

        Entrepreneurs
```

Key: (1) *Entrepreneurs were able to take the new inventions and make them into profitable businesses. This created jobs and wealth.*

a Copy the diagram into your book.

b Then draw lines between those factors that you think are connected in some way.

c Give each line a number and below your diagram, explain the connection between the factors.

To help you get started, one connection has been drawn and explained for you.

MISSION ACCOMPLISHED?

• Could you explain how different factors combined to create an Industrial Revolution?

What made Sheffield stink?

MISSION OBJECTIVES

- To understand what life was like for thousands of ordinary people in newly expanded industrial towns like Sheffield in the nineteenth century.

In 1850, the writer Charles Reade visited the town of Sheffield in the north of England. He didn't stay long! When he got home, he described Sheffield as 'perhaps the most hideous town in creation'. He reported that black smoke blocked out the sun and 'sparkling streams entered the town… but soon get filthy, full of rubbish, clogged with dirt and bubbling with rotten, foul-smelling gasses'. So what made Sheffield stink? And why had Sheffield (and many other towns like it) turned into such disgusting places to live?

Sheffield was no different to many other English towns at this time. Places such as Manchester, Leeds, Liverpool, Birmingham, Nottingham and Bolton were equally as bad. Why, then, had these towns become such horrible places to live? The answer: once a factory or two had been built, perhaps making cloth, iron or pottery, for example, people would flood in from the countryside in order to find work. The factory owners then had to build homes for the workers – usually nearby so that people could walk to work. These houses were built as quickly and as cheaply as possible, and crammed close together with narrow streets and alleys between them. Built in rows or **terraces**, the houses were also built **back-to-back** to save space and money. There was no planning or quality control and some homes were even built without foundations. In 1842, one factory owner went to visit his workers in a row of newly built houses that he rented to them and found that they had all blown down after a storm the night before.

The dramatic change in Sheffield is best illustrated by two pictures. Source A is a picture painted of Sheffield in 1750. As you can see, Sheffield looks like a peaceful place, perhaps just a bit bigger than a village. The church dominates the town and seems to be at the centre of things. Fields surround the town and there appears to be some farming going on. You should also be able to see cows, haystacks and horses.

Source B shows Sheffield about 100 years later, in the middle of the nineteenth century. It looks a lot dirtier – all smoky and polluted. Factories and terraced housing now dominate the town.

↳ **SOURCE A:** *Sheffield in 1750.*

↳ **SOURCE B:** *Sheffield around 1850.*

SOURCE F: *The upper, middle and working class. Can you work out which is which?*

Work

1 a In your own words, explain what is meant by the word 'class'.

b Describe the 'social pyramid'.

2 Study the sources about housing, education, work, leisure and food on these pages. Study the photographs especially carefully.

Imagine that you were invited to spend a day with an upper-class family and a day with a poorer family. Write a diary entry for both days, describing your experiences and feelings about your stays. Each diary entry must be longer than 50 words… but no longer than 150!

3 Look at Source D.

a Copy and label this town plan from page 60 into your book.

b Why do you think the poorer, working-class people lived near the centres of towns?

c Why do you think the richer people lived in the suburbs or out in the countryside?

—**MISSION ACCOMPLISHED?**—

• Can you describe the Victorian social pyramid – and explain how things have changed in today's society?

COULD YOU GET JUSTICE IN VICTORIAN BRITAIN?

The topic of crime and punishment is big news. The latest crime figures, the nastiest murder trials and the state of our prisons are issues that are always on our TV screens, on the radio, and in newspapers and magazines. In fact, our interest in the criminal justice system has become part of our leisure time because millions of us watch TV dramas about the police force or read books about murder investigations, infamous criminals and well-known trials. Viewing figures for the most popular TV soap operas even go up when a popular character commits a crime or faces a lengthy court case.

As a result of all the information about crime and punishment we get from our TV screens, computers, books and newspapers, people know quite a lot about law and order in today's society.

But what was the state of law and order in Victorian times? What crimes were being committed? How were criminals caught, by whom, and how severely were they punished? And what about prison life? In fact, could you get justice in Victorian Britain?

1: Law and disorder

MISSION OBJECTIVES

- To understand the state of the criminal justice system, policing, prisons and punishment in Victorian Britain and judge how they developed during the eighteenth and nineteenth centuries.

A life of crime was a very easy one in 1800. Many criminals were never caught because there were no policemen to track them down. Some places had **constables** to keep an eye on things, but these men weren't very effective. They were unpaid and were only chosen to do the job for a year before someone else took over. Many were careful not to do the job properly – they didn't want to be chosen again! Other towns had **watchmen** to keep law and order. Watchmen were paid (very badly though) and were seen as a bit of a national joke. They were often so old, or feeble, or too drunk to catch anyone that, in some areas, crime had become the number one problem.

If, by some slim chance, a criminal was caught, the law showed little mercy. Many people felt that criminals should be savagely punished so as to act as a warning to others. Indeed, in 1800, there were over 200 crimes for which a guilty person could be executed!

An amazing statistic, one which is difficult to believe today, is that one out of every eight prisoners found guilty of a crime in 1800 was sentenced to death… and the public loved to go and watch the executions. In fact, a public hanging was a day out for all the family and huge crowds turned up to watch. In 1802, 28 people were killed in a crush at a hanging outside Newgate Prison in London. Some richer people paid to rent out houses overlooking the **gallows**, and seats in specially built grandstands fetched high prices.

> Some Capital Crimes
> (Crimes for which you could be hanged)
> Theft of anything worth 5 shillings (25p) or more
> Murder, treason or piracy
> Cutting down growing trees
> Damaging Westminster Bridge
> Kidnapping
> Coining
> Stealing a sheep
> Pretending to be a pensioner of Chelsea Hospital
> Plus about 180 other crimes

'The guilty men are placed on a cart, each with a rope around his neck. The cart was driven off under the gallows. Then the criminals' friends come and pull them down by the feet so that they might die all the sooner.'

⤷ **SOURCE A:** *Adapted from* Travels in England, *by Thomas Platter, 1799.*

Yet despite the popularity of these public hangings, fewer people were hanged than should have been according to the law. Courts often took pity on young children or desperate men and women and found them not guilty… even if they had clearly committed a capital crime!

Another common punishment in 1800 was **transportation** for either five, seven or fourteen years. This meant a terrible voyage in a prison ship to a British colony, such as Australia or Gibraltar. Once there, the prisoner would become a slave, working for one of the settlers, or, perhaps, used as a worker constructing roads or buildings. After the convict had served their sentence, they were free to return to Britain. Many never did (they couldn't afford the trip home), so settled for a new life abroad.

Study these fascinating criminal cases carefully. These are real people. Their crimes and punishments have been taken from official court records.

WISE-UP Words

capital crimes
coining constable gallows
pardoned piracy
'pleads her belly'
transportation watchman

Name: Sophie Girton

Age: 25

Crime: 'She is charged with coining... that she, with Thomas Parker (aged 42), did make fake coins, mainly shillings and sixpences... and did then attempt to use them... this is an offence against the King.'

Verdict: Guilty (both of them)

Punishment: 'She is to be drawn on a hurdle to the place of execution and Sophie Girton is to be burnt.'

Notes: Her accomplice, Thomas Parker, was hanged. According to court records, it seems that Sophie Girton was possibly the last woman to be burned at the stake in England!

Name: Elizabeth Anderson

Age: 13

Crime: 'She did steal one leather bag and three silk sheets from a cloth shop... the goods were valued at ten pennies.'

Verdict: Guilty

Punishment: Whipped in the pillory and then held in Newgate Prison for one year.

Notes: It didn't matter how young you were! Criminal kids often ended up in England's filthy jails or even on prison transport ships. In 1790, ten-year-old Joe Davis was transported to Australia for stealing a pair of trousers. Punishments could be a lot worse than that, too! In 1792, a seven-year-old girl was hanged for stealing a dress; in 1802, a 12-year-old was hanged for stealing a sheep and in 1831, a nine-year-old boy was hanged for setting fire to a house.

Name: Hannah Ramsey

Age: 23

Crime: 'It is charged that she did steal a purse and a pistol valued at £2 and 5 shillings (about £2.25).'

Verdict: Guilty

Punishment: Death by hanging... 'but Ramsey pleads her belly'.

Notes: Women who claimed they were pregnant at the time they were sentenced to death could 'plead their belly'. These women (and there were lots of them) were examined by a group of women (chosen from spectators at court) and if found to be 'quick with child' (if movement of a baby was detected) their punishment was postponed until after the baby was born. Often the women were later pardoned because the court didn't want to have to deal with the problem of looking after an orphaned child. Hannah Ramsey was successful in her attempt to 'plead her belly'. Instead, she and her child were transported to Australia for seven years!

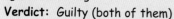

Work

1 Why were most i) constables and ii) watchmen so unreliable? Explain each answer carefully.

2 a Explain what is meant by the phrase 'capital crime'.

  b Why were so many people sentenced to death in 1800?

  c Why were fewer people executed than should have been (according to the law)?

3 Study the criminal cases carefully and answer the questions in full sentences.

  a What was Sophie Girton's crime?

  b Who do you think received the worst punishment – Sophie or her accomplice? Give reasons for your answer.

  c Why wasn't Hannah Ramsey hanged? Explain your answer carefully.

  d Was she punished at all?

  e Why do you think young Elizabeth Anderson wasn't hanged?

PAUSE for Thought

In 1793, Michael Ascot was charged with stealing 43 pairs of socks worth £3 and 10 shillings (£3.50). Why do you think the jury found him guilty of only stealing socks to the value of 4 shillings and 10d (about 24p)?

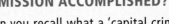

MISSION ACCOMPLISHED?

• Can you recall what a 'capital crime' is?

London had the worst crime problems because it was Britain's largest city. Naturally, then, it was the place where any crime-fighting initiative would start. In 1750, a London magistrate named Henry Fielding decided to do something about the con men, beggars, thieves and prostitutes lurking around his offices in Bow Street. He gathered six men together, gave each of them handcuffs, a pistol and a stick and promised to pay them a guinea (£1.05) a week to capture as many criminals as possible and bring them to his court. At first, they wore their own clothes but were later given a uniform. This force of thief takers became known as the Bow Street Runners.

2: Catching the vile Victorian villains

MISSION OBJECTIVES

- To be able to explain the difference between a Bow Street Runner and one of Peel's 'bobbies'.

Stick

Gun

Handcuffs

↰ **SOURCE A:** *A Bow Street Runner.*

In 1763, Henry's blind brother, John, joined the fight against crime when he set up a horse patrol to stop highwaymen on the roads in and out of London.

By 1792, seven other areas in London had set up their own versions of the Bow Street Runners. However, as crime levels kept rising and rising, it was clear to many that the country as a whole needed far more. It needed a proper police force!

The man who played a major part in creating Britain's first professional police force was an MP named Sir Robert Peel. As part of his job as the government's Home Secretary, he was responsible for dealing with law and order. In 1829, he set up the Metropolitan Police Force to replace the Bow Street Runners.

Three thousand men, mainly ex-soldiers, were enlisted into a force and each given a new blue uniform, boots, a wooden truncheon, a rattle, a brown coat and a top hat lined with iron. They received 5p a day (not much then, but better than many other jobs) and were expected to walk their 20-mile 'beat' around London, seven days a week. They had to be less than 35 years of age, healthy and able to read and write. Discipline was severe and many early recruits were sacked for drunkenness. London, with its open sewers, dirty water and filthy air, was so unhealthy that many policemen died of tuberculosis or became unfit for duty!

Steel-rimmed hat

Handcuffs

Rattle

Truncheon

To begin with, many hated the new police force. Some felt it was an invasion of privacy, a waste of money or a threat to an Englishman's freedom. Policemen were regularly beaten up in the street and spat at. Even early nicknames reflected the hostility towards them as they were branded 'Peel's bloody gang' and the 'evil blue devils'. But the 'blue devils' did a good job. They were well disciplined, good humoured and acted with restraint wherever possible (see Source D). Gradually, the public began to respect and trust them. More criminals were caught, so there was less crime in London too! Soon other towns copied London's lead and, by 1856, every town in the country had its own policemen.

SOURCE B: *A policeman, 1829. These men soon became known as 'Peelers' or 'Bobbies' after the surname or Christian name of their founder.* ↱

Who were the suspects?

A few years after the last of the murders, the man in charge of policing in Britain named his three top suspects. They were:

- M. J. Druitt – a lawyer and teacher who had trained as a doctor. Even his own family thought he might be the 'Ripper'. He killed himself in December 1888.

- Aaron Kosminski – a lunatic who heard voices and would only eat from the gutter. Police who worked for a long time on the case thought it could be him.

- Michael Ostrog – a Russian doctor who worked in a women's hospital. He went back to Russia shortly after the last murder and was eventually sent to a mental hospital for stabbing a woman in St Petersburg.

Other popular Ripper suspects include an artist named Walter Sickert, a cotton merchant named James Maybrick, an American doctor named Francis Tumblety and a barber called George Chapman, who was convicted of poisoning two of his wives. He lived in Whitechapel at the time of the murders and trained as a doctor! Over the years, many writers and historians have claimed to know who the real Ripper was… but no one has ever proved anything!

⌐ **SOURCE L:** *A 2001 film* From Hell *charts the Ripper murders and proposes Queen Victoria's grandson – Prince Albert Victor – as the main suspect. In total, there have been at least 12 Ripper films, 4 television series and over 200 books. Experts on the subject are even known as Ripperologists!*

Work

1 The following eight events have all been mixed up. Put them in the correct chronological order:
- Murder of Elizabeth Stride.
- Second 'Dear Boss' letter arrives.
- Murder of Mary Kelly.
- Murder of Mary Ann Nichols.
- Police receive letter and human body parts through post.
- Murder of Annie Chapman.
- Murder of Catherine Eddowes.
- First 'Dear Boss' letter arrives.

2 a What is meant by the term 'modus operandi'?

b In your own words, explain Jack's modus operandi.

c Can you think of any reasons why Jack chose the Whitechapel area of London to hunt for victims?

3 Look at Source K. As you can see from the wide variety of descriptions, the job of narrowing down the search for the Ripper by working out what he looked like was a very difficult one. However, there are enough similarities in some of the witness statements to give us a good idea, or a 'best fit', as to what the Ripper might have looked like. Using the witness statements, design a 'WANTED' poster for 'Jack the Ripper'.

- Draw a full length 'artist's impression'.

- Include a BEWARE file warning the public what to watch out for: physical appearance, usual clothing, approximate age, 'killing time', favourite 'haunts' and any other useful information.

TOP TIP: Make sure you do a draft copy, then a neat one on A3 paper – it will make a great class display.

__ **MISSION ACCOMPLISHED?** __

- Could you create a Fact-File on Jack the Ripper outlining your top ten facts about him?

Have you been learning? 1

TASK 1 Population and punctuation _____

The two paragraphs below don't make much sense. They need capital letters, commas, apostrophes and full stops.

a Copy the paragraphs, adding punctuation as you write.

between 1750 and 1900 the population of britain grew very fast in 1750 there were about 7 million people living in britain with another 3 million living in ireland however by 1900 britains population shot up to nearly 40 million

the places where people lived had changed too in 1750 only two out of ten people lived in towns while the rest lived in the countryside by 1900 many people had left the countryside and moved into the towns a census of 1901 showed that over 70% of people were now living in towns

b Answer the following questions:

i) Give at least five reasons why the population grew so rapidly between 1750 and 1900. Explain your reasons carefully. You might want to refresh your memory by looking at pages 10 and 11.

ii) Why did people move from the countryside to the towns?

TASK 2 The 'Factory Game' _____

As you have learned, many factories had very strict rules. Workers were fined if they didn't obey them. Play the 'Factory Game' with your friends and see who escapes with the smallest amount of fines!

You will need:

- two, three or four players
- six pieces of paper, numbered 1–6, or a die
- a blank copy each of the 'Record of Fines' sheet (see below – why not copy one out?).

RECORD OF FINES		
DAY	**OFFENCE**	**FINE**
MONDAY		
TUESDAY		
WEDNESDAY		
THURSDAY		
FRIDAY		
SATURDAY		
	TOTAL FINES	

How to play:

- The game begins on Monday. Player 1 picks a number (which should be folded up so no one can identify it!) or throws the die.
- Look at the Game Chart and read along Monday until you match your number to a letter. For example, if Player 1 throws a 2, their letter would be 'D'.
- Look up your offence on the Factory Rules notice. These are real rules and fines from a factory near Leeds in 1844.
- Fill in your fine on your Record of Fines.
- All other players choose numbers and fill in their Record of Fines for Monday.
- Move onto Tuesday and so on.

The winner:

When all fines are added together, the winner is the one with the least amount of fines.

GAME CHART						
	Number thrown					
Day of week	**1**	**2**	**3**	**4**	**5**	**6**
MONDAY	C	D	A 10 mins	F	A 5 mins	☺
TUESDAY	A 15 mins	☺	B	E	B	C
WEDNESDAY	F	F	C	A 5 mins	B	D
THURSDAY	D	☺	☺	B	C	F
FRIDAY	B	C	A 10 mins	D	E	F
SATURDAY	☺	C	D	☺	☺	A 5 mins

FACTORY RULES

A Late for work: 5 minutes = 2p fine; 10 minutes = 5p fine; 15 minutes = 10p fine

B Leaving room without permission = 3p fine

C Whistling, singing or talking = 2p fine

D Swearing or failing to follow instructions immediately = 5p fine

E Leaving the workplace in an untidy way = 2p fine

F Feeling ill and failing to find someone to do your job for you = 4p fine

☺ A good day = no fine!

Nelson's wind-powered ships could inflict terrible damage but were dangerous places to be!

Guns (A) weighed up to 3 tons and would fly backwards when fired. They had to be held in place with strong ropes to prevent the crew being crushed by their own guns.

The youngest person in Nelson's fleet was eight years old. Boys were used as **powder monkeys** (B), whose job it was to fetch the gunpowder from the **magazine** (C) and deliver it to the guns. If the bags of powder were hit by a musket ball, a boy's arm would 'disappear in a pink mist'.

Soldiers – or **marines** (D) – would try to board the enemy ship. While they fought hand-to-hand with cutlasses, tomahawks and pikes, **sharpshooters** (E) would stay on their own ships and pick off the enemy from a distance.

The only treatment available for limbs smashed by a cannon ball was amputation (F). Those that survived the ship's surgeon's saw often died of infection in the days after.

★ WISE-UP Words

ammunition   broadsides   chain shot
grape shot   magazine   marines   raking
round shot   powder monkeys
sharpshooters

Round shots were solid metal balls 15cm in diameter and the most commonly fired of all the **ammunition**. They would smash through the sides of the enemy ships, sending deadly wooden splinters flying below deck.

Grape shots were canvas bags that held gof-ball-sized lumps of metal. These would spread out when fired and could devastate a deck full of men.

Chain shots were used to destroy sails and rigging. They would also cut a man in two if he was unfortunate enough to get in their way!

↳ SOURCE A: *Types of ammunition.*

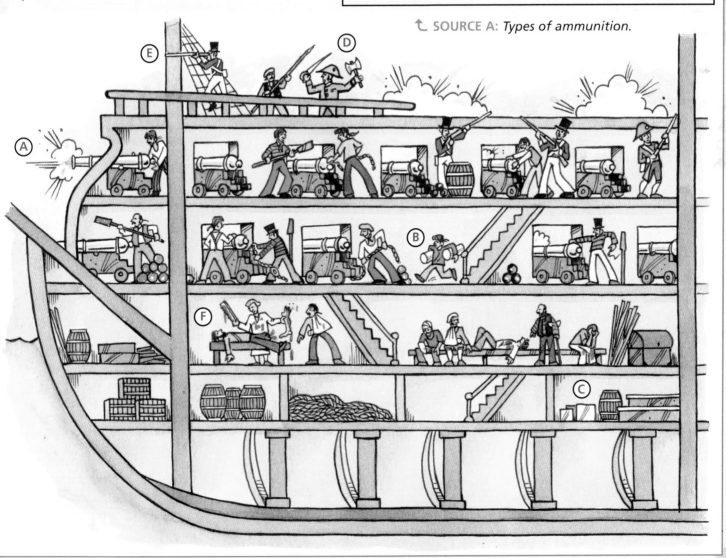

'Nelson's touch'

The traditional way of fighting at sea in the sixteenth and seventeenth centuries was for ships to sail alongside each other, firing **broadsides** and trying to board each other. This meant that battles often ended in a draw or with no clear winner. To avoid this, Nelson came up with a plan that he hoped would deal with the French and Spanish navies once and for all – it became known as the 'Nelson touch'. When he gathered his captains together and told them of his idea, he claimed: 'It was like an electric shock, some shed tears, all approved.'

The traditional attack meant that battles were often drawn – and Nelson knew he would be outnumbered when he met the French and Spanish ships.

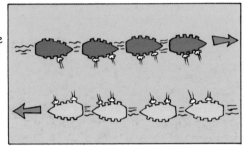

Nelson planned to break the French line at a 90° angle. This would allow his ships to fire through the length of the enemy ships – without them firing back. This was called raking.

21 October 1805 – The Battle of Trafalgar

As the French and Spanish ships left the port of Cadiz, Nelson divided his ships into two groups. He commanded one himself and gave command of the other to Admiral Collingwood. By attacking in two different places, the Royal Navy could rake through the enemy and cut the French ships at the front of the line out of the battle.

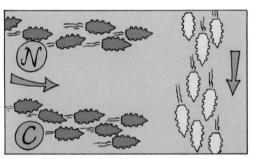

The problem with 'Nelson's touch' was that the Royal Navy was unable to fire as they approached the enemy and they sailed into a storm of shot. But once they had broken the Franco-Spanish lines, the raking British guns and superior training gave them the upper hand. Amid scenes of fierce fighting on board HMS *Victory*, Nelson was hit by a French sharpshooter. Despite this, French ships started to surrender and, at 4:15pm, the injured Nelson was told that the battle had been won. He replied, 'Now I am satisfied. Thank God, I have done my duty.' By 4:30pm, Nelson was dead.

SOURCE B: *Nelson refused to move to a safer ship or remove his medals and was an obvious target for French sharpshooters. At around 1:20pm, he was hit in the shoulder by a musket ball that lodged in his spine. Can you see him at the front-right of this picture?*

The importance of Trafalgar

As the years past, people began to see Nelson's victory over Napoleon's navies as being more and more important. Not only had it removed the threat of French invasion, it also enabled Britain to get richer and more powerful. Having control of the seas meant that Britain could trade with countries like India and China safely and without competition. This paved the way for the British Empire!

Nelson remembered – Trafalgar Square

In 1839, nearly 35 years after the battle, Parliament decided to commemorate Nelson's victory over the French. A huge square was cleared in the centre of London and a column almost 60m tall was placed in the middle of it. The square was named Trafalgar Square and a statue of Nelson was placed on top of the column. Four enormous bronze lions were also made from captured French cannons and placed at the base of Nelson's column! Trafalgar Square – with its pigeons – is now a world famous landmark and visited by millions of tourists every year.

SOURCE C: *Trafalgar Square.*

↵ **SOURCE D:** *The ship on which Nelson fought and died at Trafalgar, HMS* Victory, *is the only remaining eighteenth-century warship in the world. She is still the official flagship of the Royal Navy and has her own captain and crew.*

! FACT Roll out the barrels!

Nelson's body was put in a large barrel of brandy to stop it rotting on the way back to England! He was to be buried as a hero and his coffin was carried through huge crowds, in a carriage shaped like a battleship, before being laid to rest in a black marble crypt in St Paul's Cathedral. The nation had won a famous victory – but grieved for a lost son.

Work

1 What famous message did Nelson signal to the other ships before the battle?

2 What ammunition would you use to:
   - try and sink a ship
   - kill marines on deck
   - take down the sails and rigging.

3 In full sentences, explain the advantages and risks of 'Nelsons' touch'.

4 Imagine you are serving as a powder monkey on board HMS *Victory* on the day of the Battle of Trafalgar. Write a fictional account of all the things you did and saw that day. Remember to include plenty of historical detail and use lots of adjectives to describe what you felt, smelled, heard, witnessed, said, and so on. You may even want to include a description of Nelson's death and how the crew felt after the fighting was over.

5 Why do you think people began to see the victory at Trafalgar as a key moment in British history?

___ **MISSION ACCOMPLISHED?** ___

- Do you know how and why Nelson was celebrated as a national hero in Britain after his victory at Trafalgar?

In 1814, following defeat in Russia, Napoleon was forced to abdicate (step down) as Emperor and was held prisoner on the island of Elba by Britain, Austria, Prussia and Russia. But, determined to have one more go, Napoleon managed to escape, return to Paris and raise a new army. He marched his soldiers to Belgium where he met his arch-enemy, the Duke of Wellington, leader of a huge army of British, German, Dutch and Belgian troops. They faced each other outside the small town of Waterloo. The battle that followed has gone down in history as a famous British victory and Wellington became a national hero. But was it Wellington's leadership that won the day? Did Napoleon cause his own downfall? And what happened to Napoleon after this defeat?

3: Waterloo – Napoleon was defeated there!

MISSION OBJECTIVES

- To understand why the Battle of Waterloo was so important in the Napoleonic wars.
- To come to a conclusion over whether the battle was won or lost.

Napoleon's defeat at Waterloo meant that the French domination if Europe was finally over. Never again did Napoleon take to the battlefield. But ever since the battle, historians have argued over whether it was Wellington's brilliance or Napoleon's mistakes that caused the French defeat. Look through the following evidence and decide for yourself.

EVIDENCE A

Wellington investigated the land long before the battle began. He realised how important the three farmhouses in the middle of the battlefield would be and put some of his best soldiers in them to defend them. The French attacked them many times but failed to occupy them.

EVIDENCE B

It rained heavily on the night before the battle. The wet ground made movement slow and difficult but Napoleon ordered the attack to go ahead anyway.

EVIDENCE C

Wellington spread his **infantry** in lines just two men deep – this allowed all of the soldiers to fire their muskets.

⤶ SOURCE A: *Napoleon Bonaparte. The French Emperor had dominated Europe for nearly 20 years.*

SOURCE B: *The Duke of Wellington.*

Shako: allowed generals to identify different regiments

Brightly coloured uniform: allowed the generals to see who was on each side

Bayonet: used during hand-to-hand fighting

Musket: inaccurate and slow to load

SOURCE C: *A Napoleonic soldier.*

EVIDENCE D

When Wellington's infantry came under heavy fire from French artillery, he ordered them to move behind a ridge and lie down in long grass. This caused the French to think they were retreating and allowed the British soldiers to wipe them out as they came over the ridge.

SOURCE D: *This breast plate gives you some idea of the devastating power of artillery.*

EVIDENCE E

Napoleon felt ill and decided to leave the battlefield for a lie down. He put Marshal Ney in charge – who had a reputation for making rash decisions.

EVIDENCE G

Napoleon put all of his artillery in one place – at the front of his army. This meant they could deliver devastating firepower but couldn't reach all areas of the battlefield.

EVIDENCE F

The French infantry advanced in narrow columns that were just six men wide but many rows deep. This meant that only those at the front could fight and most of the men in the column couldn't fire their muskets.

! FACT He's legless!

During the battle, a cannon ball hit the Earl of Uxbridge as he rode next to the Duke of Wellington. The Duke said, 'By God sir, you've lost your leg!' and Uxbridge replied, 'By God sir, so I have!' The leg was amputated and buried nearby, where it became a popular tourist attraction!

EVIDENCE H

Wellington inspired his troops by putting himself in the thick of the action and only narrowly avoided being killed several times.

EVIDENCE I

The Prussian Army was rapidly marching to join up with Wellington's soldiers. Napoleon sent 30 000 of his men from the battlefield to try and stop the Prussian advance. They failed and the Prussians were soon at Waterloo, attacking Napoleon.

EVIDENCE J

Marshal Ney saw the British infantry move behind the ridge, assumed they were retreating and sent all of the French Cavalry after them. The British soldiers were hiding in the long grass and wiped out the French as they came over the ridge.

EVIDENCE K

Wellington knew that time was on his side. He took no risks and waited for the Prussians to arrive – forcing Napoleon to gamble on dangerous attacks.

SOURCE E: *Napoleon wasn't his usual energetic and inspirational self at Waterloo.* ↱

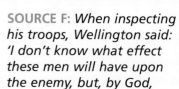

SOURCE F: *When inspecting his troops, Wellington said: 'I don't know what effect these men will have upon the enemy, but, by God, they frighten me.'* ↳

What about naughty children?

Teachers were tough – and so were punishments. Being rude, leaving school without permission, sulking, answering back, throwing ink and being late were all punishable offences.

What equipment did they use?

Younger children learned to write on slates, using slate pencils. Paper was expensive but slate could be used again and again. The students just rubbed out the letters when they'd finished. Older students used paper 'copybooks' and wrote in them with a metal-nibbed wooden pen. They dipped their nibs into ink-pots and scratched the letter onto the page. They had to be careful not to spill any ink!

SOURCE E: *These punishments were all used in British schools.*

PUNISHMENTS
Tying a student to a desk
The cane
Wearing a dunce's hat
Putting a student in a basket hanging from the roof
Hanging logs around a student's neck

WISE-UP Words

dame school
logbook
ragged school
tutor

! FACT **What about the rich kids?**

Rich boys were taught at home by private **tutors** until they were seven or eight years old. Then they went away to boarding school to learn Latin, Greek, literature, history, geography, science and sport. Rich girls stayed at home. They learned to sew, look after a home, cook, sing and play musical instruments.

‖ PAUSE for Thought

Have you ever heard of the phrase, 'You've blotted your copybook'? Where do you think it comes from?

Work

1 a What was: i) a dame school; and ii) a ragged school?

 b According to the government, why were these schools not good enough to educate Britain's children?

2 Look at Source A.

 a What were the 'three Rs'?

 b Do you think this is a sensible name for these three subjects? Explain your answer.

 c Why do you think boys and girls were taught different things in the afternoon?

3 Look at Source B.

 a Make a list of some of the major differences between the classroom in Source B and the one you are sitting in.

 b What is the biggest difference?

4 Look at Source D.

 a What is a logbook?

 b Why was Mr Brown in trouble?

 c Why was Mrs Ferguson asked to come into school?

 d Does anything surprise you about the last entry in the logbook?

5 Look at Source E.

 a Why do you think schools had punishments like these?

 b Which of these punishments do you think is the most cruel? Give reasons for your answer.

 c Why do you think the government eventually banned these punishments in British schools?

 d Should any of these punishments be re-introduced? Give reasons for your answer.

6 Imagine you are a student at the sort of Victorian school described in these four pages. You have been asked to prepare an 'induction leaflet' that will be given to all new students starting at the school. Write your leaflet, remembering to include:

• Information about the sort of lessons they'll be doing.

• Methods of teaching and learning.

• A description of a typical schoolroom.

• Some of the rules in place and what to expect if rules are broken.

• A guide to the equipment in use.

MISSION ACCOMPLISHED?

• Can you explain why there were differences between girls' and boys' timetables in Victorian schools?

• Can you describe how students were taught (and punished)?

A healthier nation?

- To understand how and why attitudes towards cleanliness changed in the nineteenth century.
- To be able to explain how surgeons won the battle against pain and infection.

Look at Source A. It is a painting from 1750. The patient is in absolute agony. Look at his face; he is being held down while the surgeon cuts off his leg. The poor man won't have been given any painkilling drugs – he is completely awake when the surgeon starts to slice into his skin and saw through his thighbone. It is highly unlikely that the medical equipment being used has ever been washed either. It will be stained with the dry blood and pus from a previous patient. One well-known surgeon used to sharpen his knives on the sole of his boot before using them. And you know how filthy the streets were! What do you think the patient's chances of survival were? Why were conditions so bad? And why have they improved so much since then?

The enemy within

In 1750, a patient in a British hospital had two major enemies. One was the pain during the operation; the other was infection afterwards. Either could kill you! Only when these two obstacles were dealt with would it be possible to make any real medical progress. In the nineteenth century, doctors started to find the solutions to these problems… and changed the way the sick were cared for forever!

Can I have something for the pain?

For hundreds of years, doctors and surgeons had tried to reduce a patient's pain during surgery. Getting them drunk or hitting them over the head were two of the most common methods. But, in 1846, an American dentist called William Morton tried out a new idea. He put his patients to sleep for a short period of time using a gas called **ether**. It worked! The patient felt no pain during the operation, woke up 20 minutes later and went home. Anaesthetics (based on the word 'ether') were born and the idea soon caught on among London's surgeons. However, ether irritated patients' eyes and made them cough and vomit during operations. So, in 1847, a Scottish doctor called James Simpson tried **chloroform** as an alternative. Again, it worked, but had less of the nasty side effects of ether. Soon, chloroform became the most common anaesthetic in the land – even Queen Victoria used it in 1853 as a painkiller while giving birth to her son, Leopold.

SOURCE A: *A painting of an amputation about to take place.* ↱

Horrible Hospitals

The use of anaesthetic was a great step forward but it didn't stop people dying from infections after operations. Today, we take it for granted that our hospitals and operating theatres are very, very clean but, in the early 1800s, it was a very different story. Hospitals were dirty places, where patients were all herded together whether they had a highly contagious fever or a broken arm. The operating theatres were no better. The only thing that was ever cleaned out was the sand box from under the operating table, which was used to catch a patient's blood during surgery. The cockroaches in St Thomas' Hospital in London were said to be the biggest in London. They fed on dried blood and dead skin. Doctors and surgeons didn't understand the need for cleanliness because they didn't know that germs caused disease. It would take a few more famous men to solve this problem!

WISE-UP Words

amputate
chloroform
ether

! FACT Record breaker

In the 1840s, a famous London surgeon named Robert Liston held the world record for **amputating** a leg – two and a half minutes. Unfortunately, he worked so fast that he accidentally cut off the patient's testicles! Also, he once cut off his assistant's fingers during another operation and a spectator dropped dead with fright.

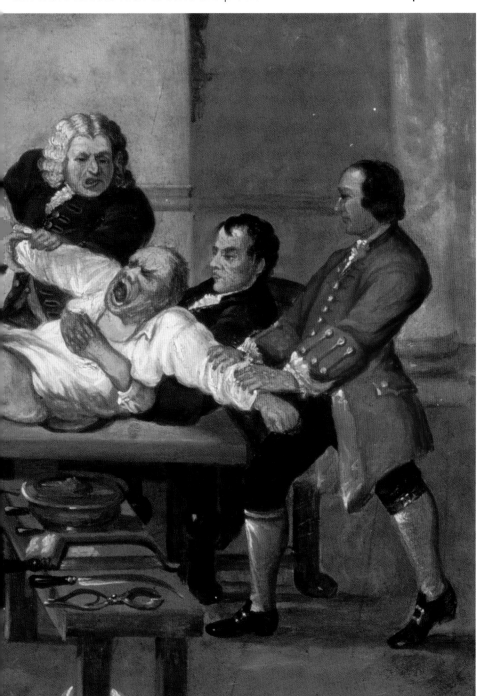

! FACT Hospitals

The word 'hospital' comes from the Latin word 'hospitale', meaning 'a place for guests'. By 1750, London had some of the finest hospitals in Europe. St Bartholomew's was the oldest but, by this time, rich men with a desire to do good things had donated money to help open many others. Westminster, Guy's, St George's Infirmary and Middlesex hospitals were all built before 1750 and, even today, still provide medical care for Britain's citizens.

Work

1 Write a short description of the scene in Source A. Use no more than 100 words.

2 Make a list of things in Source A that would not happen during an operation today.

The fight against infection

By the end of the 1850s, surgeons were able to perform much better operations. They could spend longer working on the patients because they were 'under anaesthetic' and there was no danger of them waking up and dying of pain and shock. However, people still continued to die of blood poisoning and nasty infections! After all, the doctors were operating on old wooden tables, in dirty rooms, in their ordinary clothes, using unwashed instruments that had been used on several other patients that day. Many doctors just didn't realise the danger of dirt! Read Source B carefully.

'A strong, young farmer came into the hospital and told the surgeon that his girlfriend had made comments about his nose – it was too much to one side; could it be straightened? He had heard of the wonderful things that were done in London hospitals. He was admitted; the septum (bone between the nostrils) was straightened and in five days he was dead. He died of hospital **sepsis**.'

↰ **SOURCE B:** *Visiting a hospital was a risky business (adapted from J. Leeson in* Lister as I knew him, *1927).*

Germ warfare

'Sepsis' is the Greek word for 'rotten'. The farmer's wound had gone rotten and he had died from blood poisoning (Source B). In fact, the amount of patients dying after operations in the 1850s was astonishing – as many as six out of ten! In 1864, Louis Pasteur identified tiny creatures, or germs, with his microscope. He said that some of these germs caused infection and disease. This was a major breakthrough. He went on to say that many of these germs could be killed by heat – and proved it in his laboratory. We still use '**pasteurisation**' – the heating of food and drink (check your milk carton) – to help prevent infection today.

Acid attack

In 1867, an English doctor, Joseph Lister, took Pasteur's theories one step further. He thought that it might be germs that caused so many of his patients to die from sepsis. Surely, he believed, if the germs were killed with antiseptic ('anti' means against), then more of his patients would survive. Lister chose carbolic acid as his antiseptic. Using a pump, a bit like an aerosol can, he sprayed anything that might possibly come into contact with the wound. Spray everything, he hoped, and all the germs would die. He was right! His patient didn't get any infections and antiseptics were born.

Soon doctors and surgeons all over the country were trying antiseptic sprays and other cleaner ways to work. Hospitals waged a war against germs. Walls were scrubbed clean, floors were swept and equipment was **sterilised**. Surgeons started to wear rubber gloves, surgical gowns and face masks during operations.

! FACT Vaccination

For years, Edward Jenner had observed that people with cowpox (a mild and harmless disease) didn't get smallpox (a serious killer disease). So he took pus from the blister of a girl who had cowpox and squirted it into two cuts in the arm of an eight-year-old boy named James Phipps. Next he injected Phipps with smallpox. It was a risky experiment but the boy didn't catch the deadly disease! Jenner had discovered a way of preventing smallpox, one of Britain's biggest killers. Soon doctors were calling this method **vaccination**, from '*vacca*', the Latin word for cow. By the 1880s, it was widely accepted that one way to prevent disease was to inject a weakened form of the germ in order to allow the body to build up its own defences. This is how it is done today.

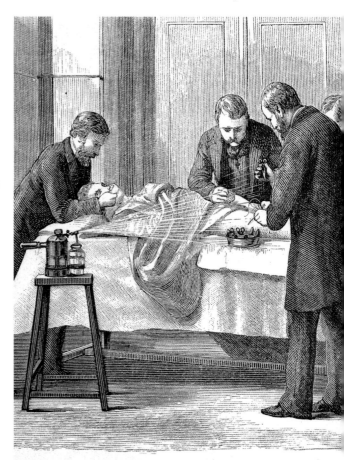

↰ **SOURCE C:** *Antiseptic in action. An operation using Lister's carbolic acid spray. Note the doctor on the left putting the patient 'to sleep' with an anaesthetic.*

The results of these measures were plain to see. Hospitals started to cure more people than they killed. Astonishingly, figures from Newcastle Infirmary, published in 1878, show that before antiseptics were introduced, six out of ten people died after operations. After antiseptics, only one out of every ten died!

Natural selection

The mystery of the different beaks stayed with Darwin and he thought long and hard about it – for the next 23 years! In 1859, he published his explanation in *The Origin of Species* – and horrified the Christian Church. Rather than being created by God, Darwin argued that all living things had **evolved** over millions of years. His **theory of evolution** suggested that the animals that were best suited to their environments would survive and reproduce. Their offspring would inherit the same features as their parents (do you look a bit like your mum or dad?) and also survive and reproduce. After thousands of years, the animals with those features become the **dominant species**. According to Darwin, which animals survived had nothing to do with God – it was down to natural selection.

★ **WISE-UP** Words

contradicted
dominant species
evolved
observation
theory of evolution

1. Geospiza magnirostris.
2. Geospiza fortis.
3. Geospiza parvula.
4. Certhidea olivacea.

FINCHES FROM GALAPAGOS ARCHIPELAGO.

↵ **SOURCE B:** *These are the finches that got Darwin thinking. Each species lived on a different island and had adapted – or evolved – depending on what food was available. This is shown by the different beak shapes: one has a broad beak for cracking seeds; one has a long curved beak for reaching down into cactus flowers; one has a short stubby beak for eating ticks off tortoises and one pecks at sea birds and feeds on their blood!*

Can you Adam and Eve it?

It was one thing arguing with the Church over where birds and animals came from, it was quite another to argue about where man came from. In 1871, Darwin did just that when he published *The Descent of Man*, in which he suggested that man had evolved gradually from apes over many thousands of years – not from Adam and Eve. He was basically suggesting that humans weren't God's special creation – they were just advanced apes! Up to this point, God was the only explanation for human existence. Darwin had come up with a new one – and it didn't involve God at all.

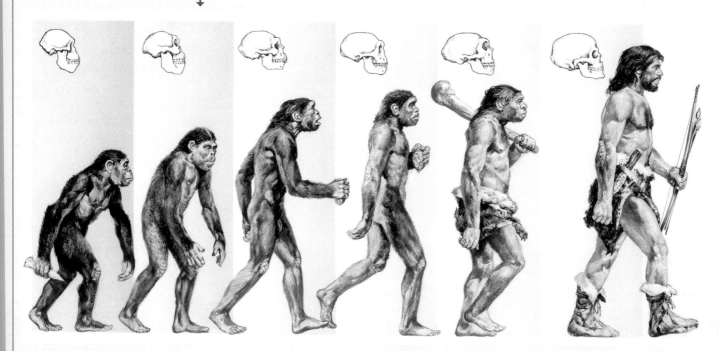

As you can imagine, the Church was far from happy about this and Darwin's ideas were attacked in books, newspapers and magazines. Not only had he come up with an idea that **contradicted** what it said in the Bible, he had come up with a simple idea that ordinary people could understand. Darwin was mocked as a madman and some even claimed his ideas were born of the Devil in order to stop people believing in God.

SOURCE D: *Darwin and his 'friend'. This drawing mocks Darwin's ideas. People at the time were not happy because he seemed to contradict the Christian faith.* ↱

✚ Hungry for **MORE**

Darwin's theory was so controversial that some states in the United States of America banned it being taught in schools. In Tennessee, it was against the law 'to teach any theory that denies the story of the Divine Creation of man as taught in the Bible and to teach instead that man has descended from animals.' In 1925, one teacher deliberately broke the law in order to make the state government prove that Adam and Eve existed. See if you can find out more about the John Scopes 'Monkey Trial' and how it ended.

'Bit by bit, I stopped believing in Christianity... I had always been told that animals were so wonderful that they must have been made by God. But now I know that animals have evolved over millions of years... I don't think we can ever know whether or not there is a god.'

↰ **SOURCE E:** *Based on the writings of Charles Darwin.*

'Are we nothing but animals? Is that what he's saying? Is religion not true? Is being good a waste of time?'

↰ **SOURCE F:** *A university professor, 1872.*

Darwin's distinguished death!

Darwin's theories remain controversial to this day and many people still strongly disagree with them. But his ideas were certainly thought provoking and seemed more and more important as the years passed. By the time he died in 1882, his work was considered so important that he was buried in Westminster Abbey alongside other great minds such as Isaac Newton and Charles Dickens. By the twenty-first century, he was seen as such an important figure that he appeared on the back of the £10 note.

Work

1 Produce your own diagram or poster that explains Darwin's theory of evolution. Use pictures where appropriate and try not to use any more than 100 words.

TOP TIP: Aim your diagram or poster at someone of your own age who has never heard of this theory before.

3 Look at Source D.

  a What point is being made by this cartoon?

  b What does this cartoon tell us about people's reactions to Darwin's theories?

4 Look at Source F. Does the professor agree or disagree with Darwin's theory of evolution? Explain how you made your decision.

5 a Why do you think Darwin was chosen to go on the £10 note?

  b If you were asked to choose a person to go on a new note, who would it be? Make sure you give sensible reasons for your choice (and it can't be yourself!).

↰ **SOURCE G:** *The Bank of England's £10 Darwin note. Who else appears on Bank of England notes? Make a list and then find out what each person has achieved.*

MISSION ACCOMPLISHED?

- Can you explain the theory of evolution?
- Could you tell someone why the Church attacked Darwin's ideas?

The birth of leisure time

MISSION OBJECTIVES

- To understand why the amount of free time (or leisure time) increased in the 1800s.
- To understand how people spent their leisure time.

Where did you spend your holidays this year? Did you stay at home? Go to a relative's house? Go to the seaside? Or were you lucky enough to go to a warm sunny place on the other side of the world?

The idea of families being able to 'go on holiday' is quite a new one. In 1800, few people had holidays. Sunday was most people's only day off, so most people rested after they had been to church. Workers were given a day off for religious festivals (Christmas Day, Easter Sunday and so on) but these 'holy days' only amounted to a couple of odd days each year.

By 1850, things had started to change. People worked shorter hours than ever before, found themselves at home earlier in the evenings and off work on Saturday afternoons. All of a sudden, ordinary workers had enough leisure time to enjoy new sports and other pastimes, or even go away for short holidays to the seaside.

In 1871, Parliament introduced bank holidays, giving workers a few more days off throughout the year when banks and offices closed. Many people found themselves asking the question that they had never asked before: 'What am I going to do with my leisure time?'

SOURCE A: *An audience and actors at a 'penny gaff', a music hall to which the admission was a penny.*

A trip to the theatre

Without television, cinemas or games consoles, people had to go out to the theatre or a musical hall to get their entertainment. There were posh theatres for listening to Shakespeare or opera, and cheaper ones for listening to **melodramas**. Melodramas were plays with really dramatic plots and lots of songs. A bit like a pantomime today, the audience were encouraged to boo and hiss at the villain and cheer for the hero.

Even cheaper than the cheap theatres were the **music halls**. The first one, 'The Canterbury', opened in London in 1851 and, soon, lots of them were built all over the country. Music halls put on a wide variety of acts including singers, comedians, acrobats, musicians and magicians. The audience sang along with songs they recognised and shouted rude comments at performers they didn't like. Some music hall performers they didn't like and others became the superstar celebrities of their day. Singing star Marie Lloyd, for example, was mobbed when she appeared in public. She is most famous for singing *My Old Man (Said Follow the Van)* and *A Little of What You Fancy Does You Good*.

Shall we go to the pub?

When ordinary people had any time off work, many of them went to their local pub and drank heavily. In London, one house in every 77 was a pub and in parts of Newcastle there was one pub for every 22 families.

⭐ **WISE-UP** Words

melodramas
music halls

FACT One pinch or two?

In order to make people thirsty for more beer, landlords would often put salt in their drinks. Interestingly, pubs today still try to encourage us to drink more by selling 'salty snacks' such as peanuts and crisps.

↰ SOURCE B: *A pub – or 'gin palace' as they were sometimes called – in the 1800s. It was a place to drink, fight, sing, gossip and gamble. Note the small child drinking too. Something that was perfectly legal at the time.*

New crazes

Photography, reading comic books, cross-stitching (a type of embroidery), cycling, roller skating, having a 'shampoo' and head massage in a bath house, and listening to musicians in a bandstand at the local park were all popular in the 1800s. Reading books become more common too, as more people learned to read. New novels by authors such as Charles Dickens (who wrote *Oliver Twist*), Jane Austen (*Pride and Prejudice*), Robert Louis Stevenson (*Treasure Island*), Lewis Carroll (*Alice's Adventures in Wonderland*) and Mary Shelley (*Frankenstein*) sold thousands of copies.

New sports

Sport became more and more popular throughout the nineteenth century. Croquet was popular in the 1860s, then tennis in the 1870s, then hockey, golf and snooker. Sport became more organised too, as standard rules were introduced across the country. Competitions soon followed: the FA Cup began in 1871, Wimbledon Tennis Championship was first played in 1877 and English and Australian cricket teams played the first Test match in England in 1880.

↰ **SOURCE C:** *A copy of* The Jungle Book, *written by Rudyard Kipling in 1894. The Disney film of the same name is based on this book.*

↰ **SOURCE D:** *After the invention of the Rover safety bicycle in 1885, cycling became a national craze. By 1900, there were thousands of cycling clubs throughout Britain.*

Blood sports

Betting on fighting animals – called '**blood sports**' – had been popular for centuries but began to die out in the 1800s. The RSPCA was set up in 1824 and bear baiting and cockfighting became illegal in 1849.

A day at the seaside

The growth of the railways meant that ordinary people were able to travel away from the towns or the countryside. People would save up all year so they could go to coastal towns like Blackpool, Brighton, Southend or Margate. Hotels, amusement arcades, piers and promenades were built to entertain the thousands of 'day trippers' who travelled to these seaside towns in search of fun. And one of the first to realise that there was money to be made by organising rail trips to Britain's beaches was a man called Thomas Cook in the 1840s. It wasn't long before he was organising week-long holidays too. The company he created still organises holidays today.

! FACT The rich
The upper classes had always enjoyed plenty of leisure time. It was usual for the children of rich families, for example, to spend six months or more doing a 'Grand Tour' of Europe's capital cities after they had left school.

SOURCE E: *Ramsgate beach in July 1887. Can you see:*
i) the pier?
ii) the Punch and Judy show?
iii) the ice-cream seller?
iv) the seafront hotels?
v) the 'bathing booths' (a sort of portable changing room that swimmers wheeled out into the sea)?
vi) the railway station, which brought visitors right up to the sea front? ⤵

WISE-UP Words

blood sports

Work 〰

1 a What is 'leisure time'?

 b Why did the amount of leisure time enjoyed by many people start to increase after 1850?

2 a What were 'blood sports'?

 b Why do you think these 'sports' gradually began to disappear?

3 Look at Source E.

 a Write a short description of this scene.

 b In what ways is the beach at Ramsgate in 1887 different from a typical British seaside beach today?

4 It is 1890. Plan a weekend's entertainment for you and your friend and write them a letter explaining how you will both spend your time:

- Will you watch any sports? If so, which ones?

- What about a day at the seaside? How will you get there? Which resort? What will you do?

- After visiting church, how will you spend Sunday afternoon? A walk in the park perhaps? What can you expect to do (and see) there?

TOP TIP: You want to make your friend excited about their visit, so your letter should be enthusiastically written!

___**MISSION ACCOMPLISHED?**___

- Could you explain at least five ways in which an ordinary person might spend their leisure time in the 1800s?

- Can you compare these with how you spend your leisure time today?

A sporting nation

MISSION OBJECTIVES

- To be able to explain how, when and why Britain's obsession with sport began.
- To identify how the Industrial Revolution helped.

In Britain today, millions of people play some sort of organised sport every week. It might be football, athletics, cricket, dance or even fishing. Millions more watch sporting events on television or may attend the matches of their favourite team in person – many even have a season ticket. If you had mentioned sport to somebody in the eighteenth century, they would have assumed you were talking about shooting a bird or hunting a fox with dogs. But, by 1900, all sorts of new sports that captivated the nation had been invented and were soon being played all around the world. So how did the idea of sport change so dramatically? Why did it turn into such a major part of our lives? And how and when did this happen?

I don't like cricket – I love it!

Nobody is exactly sure about when and where the game of cricket was first played but the first evidence of adults playing comes from 1611 – when two men were punished for having a game instead of going to church! Large games were organised in the 1700s but mainly as an excuse to place huge bets. The Marylebone Cricket Club was formed in 1787 but it was in the following century that the game really took off and saw the creation of today's county clubs and rules. The railways enabled players and supporters to travel to other cities for matches and, in 1873, the County Championship began. The British Empire meant that the game was exported overseas and the first international test match was played between England and Australia in Melbourne in 1877 – the Aussies won. When the Australian team visited England in 1882, they emerged as winners once more, causing *The Times* newspaper to write this obituary:

> In Affectionate Remembrance
> of
> **ENGLISH CRICKET,**
> which died at the Oval
> on
> 29th A U G U S T, 1882,
> Deeply lamented by a large circle of sorrowing friends and acquaintances
> R.I.P.
> N.B. – The body will be cremated and the ashes taken to Australia.

The following year, the England team visited Australia and the captain was given a small urn containing the ashes of the bails from the previous game. From that day on, whenever England and Australia play each other, they play for possession of 'The Ashes'.

SOURCE A: *'The Ashes' urn.* ↱

↰ **SOURCE B:** *A cricket match between Sussex and Kent.*

Anyone for tennis?

Like cricket, the exact origins of tennis have been lost in the mists of time. The modern sport can trace its roots to a game that was very popular with French aristocrats in the sixteenth, seventeenth and eighteenth centuries called Real Tennis. Players would begin the game by shouting 'Play' (or 'Tenez' in France) and then hitting a ball over a net. But Real (or Royal) Tennis is played indoors and the court is surrounded by walls, which the players can bounce the ball off. The scoring system of 15, 30, 40 and then 'game', which is still used today, is thought to come from the value of coins used in sixteenth-century France. When a player has no points, it is still referred to as 'love' by the umpire. This comes from the French for 'the egg' (*l'oeuf*), which is what the number zero looks like when it's written down!

The need for a special indoor court meant that only the very rich could afford to play – but all that changed in the 1800s. Well-off Victorians had huge flat lawns in front of their houses and were eager for a game to play on them. Croquet was very popular at first but the invention of the soft rubber ball meant that tennis could now be played without damaging the grass. Lawn Tennis soon caught on and, in 1877, the All England Croquet Club (formed in Wimbledon in 1868) decided to allow some of their lawns to be used for a tennis competition. The final was delayed by four days due to heavy rain and a crowd of 200 watched local man Spencer Gore beat William Marshall 6–1, 6–2, 6–4. Despite being crowned the first Wimbledon champion, Gore wasn't a massive fan, describing tennis as 'a monotonous game compared with others'! The game of Lawn Tennis is now hugely popular all around the world and Wimbledon, which is the only major competition that still uses grass courts, is seen as the most important tournament a tennis player can win.

↳ **SOURCE C:** *Tennis was the perfect sport to use the large Victorian lawns.*

Scotland gets teed off!

The game of golf, which is now played and watched by millions of people all over the planet, owes its existence to Scotland and the advances of the Industrial Revolution. Balls made of wood, and, later, leather and feathers, had been hit around the countryside with wooden clubs by Scottish noblemen in the 1700s. But the price of the balls (which were more expensive than the clubs) and access to the land meant that only a few people could play it. All that changed in 1848 when the gutta-percha ball – or 'gutty' – was invented by a Scottish vicar called James Patterson. Gutta percha is like rubber but harder and comes from the sap of trees found in South-East Asia. The expansion of the British Empire meant it soon came to Scotland, where Patterson heated and then moulded it into balls. Gutty balls could be made quickly and cheaply, meaning more people could now afford to play. They were also much stronger – meaning they could be hit harder and more accurately with the new iron clubs. In 1851, the first purpose-built golf course in the world was opened in Prestwick, Scotland. When the railways came to St Andrews in 1852, people flooded north – just to play golf! In 1860, the first Open was held and the winner received a red leather belt! Golf's popularity meant courses soon started to pop up all over Britain and then the world.

↳ **SOURCE D:** *The golf course at St Andrews today.*

Why did it all kick off?

Football is now a hugely popular sport and the top players are world-famous millionaires. You may already know that football isn't a new thing and a very brutal version was played back in the Middle Ages. But it was during the nineteenth century that the modern game was created and the British public was first gripped by the 'beautiful game'. At the beginning of that century, the game was played according to rules decided on the day of the match. These differed wildly according to where you were, although some public schools had set down regular rules for themselves. The first club, Sheffield FC, was formed in 1857 and the first professional club (which paid its players) was Notts County in 1862. Others soon followed and, in 1863, the Football Association (FA) published the 'Laws of the Game'. Once these had been set, teams sprang up all over the country – especially in the new industrial towns. In 1871, the FA came up with the idea of a knockout competition so that all of these teams could play each other and the first FA Cup was held.

	P	W	D	L	F	A	Pts
Preston North End	22	18	4	0	74	15	40
Aston Villa	22	12	5	5	61	43	29
Wolverhampton Wanderers	22	12	4	6	50	37	28
Blackburn Rovers	22	10	6	6	66	45	26
Bolton Wanderers	22	10	2	10	63	59	22
West Bromwich Albion	22	10	2	10	40	46	22
Accrington	22	6	8	8	48	48	20
Everton	22	9	2	11	35	46	20
Burnley	22	7	3	12	42	62	17
Derby County	22	7	2	13	41	60	16
Notts County	22	5	2	15	39	73	12
Stoke	22	4	4	14	26	51	12

⬆ **SOURCE E:** *The final standings for the first ever football league. It was such a success that a second and third division were soon formed.*

↵ **SOURCE F:** *Arthur Wharton (1865–1930) was the world's first professional black footballer. He played professional cricket too! Born in Cannock, Staffordshire, he also held the world record for the 100-yard sprint between 1886 and 1887.*

Date	Event
1866	Ball size fixed
1870	Only 11 players allowed per team
1872	Referee first used (but only to keep time)
1872	First international between England and Scotland
1873	Free kick awarded for handball
1874	First use of shin pads
1874	Referees given power to send off players
1875	Crossbar used instead of tape
1878	Referees used whistle for the first time
1878	First floodlit match
1882	Two-handed throw-in introduced
1885	Highest ever score recorded in a British game. Arbroath beat Bon Accord in the Scottish Cup 36–0
1889	Ball weight fixed
1891	Goal nets used for the first time
1891	Penalty kick introduced

⬆ **SOURCE G:** *The laws of Association Football (as it is correctly known – and the word soccer comes from the word association) continue to change to this day. Here are some key changes in its early development.*

In 1874, Parliament passed a law which gave many workers Saturday afternoon off – leading to an explosion of new clubs. Many churches organised teams in order to stop young lads getting into trouble in their spare time and created clubs like Everton, Southampton and Aston Villa. Many other clubs came from factory sides. In 1878, workers at the Lancashire and Yorkshire Railway Company's engine depot set up a club called Newton Heath and, in 1886, workers at the Royal Arsenal in Woolwich formed their own team. These were later to become Manchester United and Arsenal Football Clubs – two of the most famous clubs in the world today.

A league of their own

The first football league was set up by 12 'founding' clubs in 1888. It was a massive success and, with workers having Saturday afternoon off, the matches drew huge crowds. The railways enabled 'fans' to travel to matches and they could keep up with their team's fortunes through the national newspapers. The fact that very little equipment was needed and that it could be played in any weather meant that even the poorest could afford to play and it soon became known as the 'people's game'. Its popularity was confirmed in 1901, when a massive crowd of over 110 000 watched the FA Cup final.

Rugby football

The game of rugby shares the same origins as the game of football. As we have already learned, some public schools set down their own version of rules for football – and one such school was Rugby. According to legend, in 1823, a student named William Webb-Ellis picked up the ball and ran with it. The school adapted their rules to allow handling and running with the ball – and 'Rugby football' was born! Other public schools soon started to use the rules devised at Rugby and, in 1871, the Rugby Football Union (RFU) was formed. This enabled grown men to carry on playing their favourite school sport and it was soon being played around the world. Over the years, people have adapted the rules and created the alternative games of 'Rugby Union', 'Rugby League', 'Australian Rules Football' and 'American Football'.

↵ **SOURCE H:** *This statue was placed outside Rugby school in William Webb-Ellis' honour, because: 'with fine disregard for the rules of football as played in his time at Rugby school, he first took the ball in his arms and ran with it, thus originating the distinctive feature of the Rugby game'.*

Work

1 The following are all key dates in the history of sport in Britain. Put them in order and explain what happened in each year.
1873 • 1882 • 1877 • 1860 • 1857 • 1862 • 1863 • 1823 • 1871 • 1888

2 Write a sentence explaining why you think so many of today's popular sports were created in Britain during the eighteenth and nineteenth centuries.

3 Divide your page into two. Give one side the title: 'Working-class sports' and the other 'Upper-class sports'. Write the name of each sport discussed under the column to which you think it belongs and explain why you have put it there.

4 Which is the most popular of these sports today? Why do you think this is?

5 Research the story behind a sports team that is local to your school. When was it formed? Who by? Why? Have they ever won anything?

—— MISSION ACCOMPLISHED? ——

- Could you tell somebody about the origins of cricket, tennis, golf, football and rugby?
- Can you explain how the Industrial Revolution made this possible?

The High Street

────────── **MISSION OBJECTIVES** ──────────

• To understand what a typical Victorian high street might have looked like.

By 1900, about 80% of the population lived in towns or cities… and they all needed a place to shop! It wasn't long before 'high-street shopping' became common.

This painting, by Louise Rayner, is called *Eastgate Street at the Cross*, (Chester). It is a great example of what a Victorian city high street would have looked like. The labels below this painting will help you to understand what's going on.

↳ **SOURCE A:** *Look out for the following:*

i) Pavements – from the 1850s, many high-street pavements were improved. The first street cleaners were employed by 1860.

ii) The tramlines – horse-drawn tramcars ran on fixed rails along the cobblestone streets. By 1890, electric trams replaced the horse-drawn ones.

iii) Street traders – as well as the shops, people could buy from street traders or **costermongers**, as they were known. Can you see the costermongers in the painting? There are at least two.

iv) Shops – how many different types of shop can you see?

v) Street lights – in high streets by 1835.

vi) Rich men, poor men – the high street was a mixture of all types of people. Can you see the upper-class men having a chat? What about the poor boys (one looking bored; the other staring through a shop window)?

New high-street shops

Up until the 1800s, goods were mainly sold in separate shops, for example, each selling just shoes, hats, coats, ribbons, underwear or shirts. But by the middle of the century, a few shops began to grow into what we call department stores, selling lots of goods under one roof. Some, like Debenhams and John Lewis, still exist today.

The 1800s was the time for the birth of many of our familiar high-street shops. William Henry Smith (1848), John Sainsbury (1869), Jesse Boot (1871), Michael Marks and Tom Spencer (1894) all started trading at this time. Thomas Lipton, a grocer, once said, 'Secret of my success? There isn't one, just advertise, advertise all you can. Never miss a chance of advertising.'

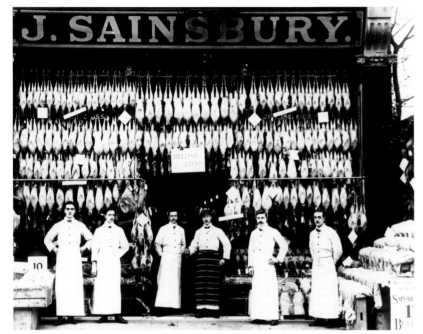

↳ **SOURCE B:** *An early Sainsbury's store. By 1880, the invention of* **refrigeration** *meant that meat could be shipped from Australia and New Zealand without going mouldy. 'Fridges' inside shops meant that meat, milk and fish could be stored easily.*

New ideas on the high street

In 1844, 28 workers from Rochdale, Lancashire, each saved up to buy a stock of food and open a shop of their own. Workers sold their goods at fair prices and shared the profits out amongst their customers. Their co-operation with each other gave its name to their first shop – 'The Co-operative'. Today, 'Co-ops' exist all around the country.

In about 1850, some shops began to sell ready-to-wear clothes. You could then literally 'buy off the peg' and take it home to wear straight away; rather than having to order your clothes first and then go back in six weeks when they had been made for you.

High-street quality

In 1875, the Sale of Food and Drugs Act made it possible for local councils to check on the quality of food on sale. The first inspectors found some amazing tricks of the trade being used by shop owners to fool their customers (like mixing river water with milk and putting sawdust into flour). Gradually, food quality improved.

WISE-UP Words

costermonger
refrigeration

Work

1 a List some of the well-known shops that appeared in Victorian high streets between 1848 and 1894.

b According to Thomas Lipton, what was the secret of his success?

c Do you think this 'secret' still applies to most large stores today? Explain your answer.

2 a How did 'The Co-operative' chain of stores get its name?

b How did the 1875 Sale of Food and Drugs Act make things safer for customers?

c How did the invention of refrigeration help: i) shop owners; and ii) customers?

3 Prepare a guidebook for the gallery in which Louise Rayner's painting hangs. You are to write the notes that would go in the guidebook:

- Start with a basic description.

- Explain what the painting tells the viewer about life in Victorian Britain – use details from the scene to help you.

- Write why it is important to look after and preserve paintings like this.

↳ **SOURCE C:** *An early 'Co-op' shop in London.*

___ **MISSION ACCOMPLISHED?** ___

- Can you describe (in more than 100 words) the sights and smells that you might have expected to find on a typical Victorian high street?

Have you been learning? 2

TASK 1 Looking closely

Below is a very famous drawing by an artist called William Hogarth. It was drawn in 1751 and is called *Gin Lane*. It shows the dangers of drinking cheap gin, a drink that was readily available between 1750 and 1850.

Look for:

i) the drunk mother dropping her baby

ii) the dead alcoholic whose dog is sitting next to him

iii) the entrances to two pubs, shown by gin tankards hanging over the doors

iv) the desperate (and poor) man and woman trying to sell their pots and pans to get money for gin. The shop is a pawnbroker's and people would sell their goods during the week and buy them back when they were paid!

v) gin being fed to a baby

vi) the drunk men playing around in a wheelbarrow

vii) the dead man being lowered into his coffin – what do you think has caused his death?

viii) the dead man hanging by a rope inside his house – was it suicide perhaps? If so, why might he have killed himself?

ix) the house about to fall on those below – was money spent on gin rather than repairs?

x) the man sharing his bone with a dog – is he too poor to eat properly… or is he too drunk to care?

a Why do you think Hogarth drew this picture?

b Do you think it got the message across about the dangers of drinking gin? Explain your answer carefully.

c Imagine you have been given the job of writing about the drawing for inclusion in a gallery's guidebook. Write a short description of *Gin Lane*. Include facts and figures about the drawing (artist, date, topic) and several features to look out for. You must not use more than 150 words!

118

TASK 2 Suffixes

A suffix is a letter or group of letters added to the end of a word. Suffixes can turn nouns into adjectives. They sometimes involve changing the spelling of the original word.

Turn the nouns in the following sentences into adjectives by adding the correct suffix from the list below:
y • ic • ous • ful • al.

a The gunpowder used in the Napoleonic wars made battlefields very **smoke**.

b In big towns, the pollution from factories meant the sky was dark – even on **sun** days.

c Many people thought that Horatio Nelson was a **hero** leader.

d Advances in science during this period made the world less **mystery**.

e In history, it is sometimes difficult to tell who is being **truth**.

f People at the Rainhill trials thought the Rocket was **marvel**.

g Locomotives were faster than even the most **athlete** horse.

h Industry thrived in the Midlands because of its **centre** location.

TASK 3 Describing pictures

One of these pictures of Manchester was painted in 1750 and the other was painted in the 1850s.

a Write a paragraph explaining which you think is which.

b Write down five adjectives that describe each picture.

BRITAIN ABROAD

People in Britain had been travelling and trading with countries overseas since the sixteenth century. But between 1750 and 1900 Britain began to take control of other countries and claim them as British property. By 1900, Queen Victoria ruled over 13 million square miles of territory – about a quarter of the world's surface – and was the head of the biggest empire the world had ever seen. The British Empire was to have dramatic effects on the lives of millions of people – both at home and abroad.

1: The Empire on which the sun never sets

MISSION OBJECTIVES

- To be able to list at least five countries that were ruled by Britain in 1900.
- To be able to explain why Britain began to take control of land and people abroad.

Look at Sources A and B. One shows the countries controlled by Britain (known as the British Empire) in 1765; the other shows the Empire in 1900. As you can see, it expanded massively between these years – but why? What made Britain want to control other countries? How was a small island in Europe able to rule over a quarter of the globe? And what part did the Industrial Revolution play in all this?

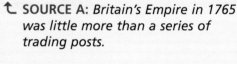

⬑ **SOURCE A:** *Britain's Empire in 1765 was little more than a series of trading posts.*

↵ **SOURCE B:** *By 1900, it covered 13 million square miles.*

Trading places

Britain's Empire began when Queen Elizabeth I allowed companies to travel the world and trade goods under her name. Merchants set up trading posts in foreign lands and started to make big profits buying and selling goods. The **raw materials** found abroad, such as, cotton, rubber and tea, were essential for Britain's factories and wealth. In order to protect the supply of these goods, many traders decided to use Britain's money and superior weapons to take over the local area as rulers. This happened in India, where the honourable East India Company gradually took control of large areas of land from more and more Indian princes. Eventually, all of India (which included Pakistan, Bangladesh and Sri Lanka) became part of the British Empire and Queen Victoria was given the title Empress of India.

Get off my land!

Britain may have been the first country in the world to go through an Industrial Revolution – but it wasn't the last (see Source C). Other European countries, such as France, started to look around the world for their own **colonies** that could supply them with raw materials. This led to wars between European nations over who controlled different parts of the world. Britain took over land held by the French, Spanish and Dutch in the Caribbean, French land in Canada, and Dutch land in Sri Lanka and South Africa. At other times, Britain fought wars against countries like Burma, Malaysia and Afghanistan to protect their existing colonies.

Country	Date of Industrial Revolution
Britain	1780
France	1830
Germany	1850
USA	1865
Japan	1890

⌐ SOURCE C: *Other countries soon followed Britain's lead when it came to manufacturing goods in factories.*

Look what I've found!

Britain also increased its Empire through exploration. People, such as David Livingstone, travelled deep into Africa to places that Europeans had never been to before. Merchants and settlers soon followed him and Britain took control of vast parts of Africa after 1870. Captain Cook landed in Botany Bay, Australia, in 1770 and claimed it for Britain. Convicts from Britain were transported the enormous distance and many settled there after their release. In 1840, Britain also 'took over' New Zealand.

WISE-UP Words

colonies
raw materials

Colonies	Raw materials
Africa	Gold, diamonds, cotton, corn, vegetable oil, copper
Australasia	Wool, meat, copper, gold, dairy produce
British Guiana	Copper
Canada	Gold, corn, wood, fish
India	Tea, cotton, wood, rubber, spices, dyes, coffee
West Indies	Sugar, rum

⌐ SOURCE D: *These raw materials were essential to keep Britain fed and its factories running.*

Work

1 Name three other European countries that Britain competed for colonies with.

2 Name the countries that Britain sourced the following raw materials from:
sugar, cotton, gold, tea, wool, coffee, copper, rubber, vegetable oil and spices.

3 Write a few sentences explaining why Britain's Empire was so important for the Industrial Revolution to continue.

4 Look at the map of the British Empire in 1900. Why do you think people started to call it the 'Empire on which the sun never sets'?

—— **MISSION ACCOMPLISHED?** ——

• Can you name five countries that once belonged to the British Empire?

• Can you give at least two reasons why Britain began to take control of other countries?

The people who became part of the British Empire were not always happy about it. More often than not, land was claimed for Britain at the point of a musket. Sometimes, Britain's soldiers won famous victories; other times, they suffered humiliating defeats. So where in the world did Britain's soldiers go to war? What countries were defeated? And what countries sent the British packing?

2: Wars of the Empire

MISSION OBJECTIVES

- To be able to explain how Britain won or lost control of at least three of its colonies.

Africa

British slave traders had been taking Africans to America since Tudor times but Britain started to take much more interest in the continent in the nineteenth century. Queen Victoria's armies fought a number wars there, both against Africans and European settlers from other countries. In 1880 and 1899, they fought against the descendents of Dutch settlers (known as **Boers**) for control of South Africa and its gold and diamond mines. In both wars, the modern, well-equipped British Army suffered humiliating defeats by armies made up of simple farmers and lost over 20 000 men. Eager for more land, in 1879 Britain started a war against Zululand – a country that was next door to the South African colonies. A quick and easy victory was expected against the Zulus who were armed merely with simple shields and spears. But the ferocious Zulu warriors overwhelmed the invading troops and an entire British army was wiped out at the Battle of Isandlwana. Following both the Boer and Zulu wars, huge amounts of money and thousands of reinforcements meant that South Africa remained part of the British Empire. Between 1880 and 1900, European countries divided up most of the continent between themselves in the 'scramble for Africa'. Britain ended up controlling 16 African colonies.

The Battle of Isandlwana.

India

The East India Company's trading posts at Surat, Madras, Bombay and Calcutta turned into major cities and were the key to Britain gaining control of India. The Company had its own army and navy and used them against the various regional rulers of India. At the Battle of Plassey in 1757, 3000 Company troops (2200 were Indians) defeated a combined Indian and French force of over 40 000. Much of the victory was due to the bribing of Indian generals but it meant that Bengal – the richest part of India – was run and controlled by the East India Company. Over the following decades, the various Indian princes and rulers were played against each other, more wars were fought and more land came under the control of the Company. In 1857, the Indian soldiers (who made up 80% of the Company's army) mutinied over the use of pork and beef fat in their rifle cartridges. This led to the British government taking direct control of India. A viceroy was placed in charge of the country and Victoria became Empress of India. To many people in Britain, India, with its huge population and wealth of raw materials, was the most important colony of them all. It became known as the 'jewel in the crown'.

Afghanistan

The East India Company didn't have everything their own way. In 1838, they sent an army of around 16 000 to Afghanistan (which is next to India) to increase their grip on the region. Although they managed to capture the capital, Kabul, and put their own man in charge, the Afghans kept attacking and killed the top British general and paraded his chopped up body through the streets. The rest of the Company's army decided it was time to leave in 1842 but were attacked all the way back to India. Of the 16 000 plus that set out on the retreat, only one man – William Brydon – made it back to the British base at Jalalabad! The invasion of Afghanistan has gone down as one of the greatest disasters in British History.

This picture is called Remnants of an Army *and shows William Brydon – the sole survivor of a 16 000-strong force – reaching Jalalabad.*

North America

Britain had had colonies in North America since the reign of James I and, by 1750, there were 13 separate British colonies in what is now called the USA. Many people had moved from Britain to live in these colonies and, by 1773, they had begun to become frustrated by being ruled from London. They were forced to pay large taxes to the British government but weren't allowed a say in any decisions that it made. British imports of tea were thrown into the sea as a protest during the Boston Tea Party and, on the 4th July 1776, the Americans declared their **independence** from Britain. Parliament sent an army to regain control but, after five years of fighting, the American War of Independence was over. The 13 colonies joined together to form the United States and, in 1789, America appointed its first President, George Washington. This valuable colony was lost forever!

Australia and New Zealand

Although Captain Cook reached Australia in 1770 and claimed it for Britain – there were already thousands of people living there! The British believed these natives, known as **Aborigines**, were inferior because they lived simple lives that were in tune with the environment around them. In some cases, the Aborigines were hunted and killed like animals – for fun. When the British reached the Australian island of Tasmania in 1802, there were 20 000 Aborigines living there. Eighty years later, there was not a single one left.

Australia was used as a prison from 1788 and thousands of convicts were taken there. In the 1850s, gold was discovered and many British people moved there to make their fortune. By 1900, there were about 4 million Europeans living in Australia.

Although Captain Cook had also sailed to New Zealand, he didn't claim it for Britain. The New Zealand Company, based in London, traded with the natives, known as Maoris, and made large profits selling guns. In 1840, there were rumours that the French were going to seize control of the islands, so the British persuaded the Maori chiefs to sign over their country to Queen Victoria. When the Maoris tried to change their minds, they felt the full force of the British Army and, during wars with the various tribes, the Maori population was reduced from 100 000 to around 35 000.

Work

1 Copy the following years into your book and place them in chronological order:

1880 • 1757 • 1857 • 1879 • 1776 • 1842 • 1840 • 1770 • 1789.

2 For each year, write a couple of sentences explaining what important event or battle took place.

3 List as many reasons as you can explaining why some people around the world believe that the British Empire was a bad thing.

WISE-UP Words

Aborigines

Boers

independence

—— MISSION ACCOMPLISHED? ——

• Can you explain how Britain won or lost control of at least three of its colonies?

In the first half of the nineteenth century, most British people would have known very little about the British Empire. It was only there to provide raw materials and make profits for the shareholders, after all. But towards the end of the century, people's attitudes to the Empire began to change. British people began to take pride in the Empire and believed it gave Britain the important responsibility of 'civilising' the people who lived in it. In the years that have followed, many people have claimed that the Empire was racist and exploited other countries just to make Britain rich. So just why did people become proud of the Empire? Why do others think it is something to be ashamed of? And what is your opinion on Britain's colonial past?

3: An Empire to be proud of?

MISSION OBJECTIVES

- To understand how the British Empire has been interpreted in different ways.
- To decide whether Britain had an Empire to be proud of.

Over the years, people have interpreted the British Empire in different ways. Some believe it was a force for good that improved the lives of the people who were part of it. Others think it was intolerant, racist and exploited people for Britain's gain. Read through the sources and see what you think.

'Ceylon (now Sri Lanka) was unified under British rule in 1815. Over the next 80 years, the British built 2300 miles of road and 2900 miles of railway. The land used for farming increased from 400 000 acres to 3.2 million acres, the schools from 170 to 2900, the hospitals from 0 to 65… .'

↰ **SOURCE A:** *Written by James Morris in* Pax Britannica, *1968.*

'Either you treat the natives as equals or call them a subject race. I have made up my mind. The native is to be treated as a child and denied the vote.'

↰ **SOURCE B:** *From a speech made by Cecil Rhodes, Prime Minister of Cape Colony (South Africa) in 1894.*

'The condition of Africa when Europe entered the continent was deplorable. On the East Coast, Arabs… were engaged in a lucrative trade in slaves for export to Arabia… . In the west, powerful armies of Moslem States depopulated large districts in their raids for slaves. … inter-tribal war was an ever-present condition of native life, and that extermination and slavery were practised by African tribes upon each other.

It was the task of civilisation to put an end to slavery, to establish Courts of Law, to… [teach] the natives a sense of liberty, and of justice, and to teach their rulers how to apply these principles… . I am confident that the verdict of history will award high praise to the achievements of Great Britain in the discharge of these great responsibilities. … under no other rule… does the African enjoy such a measure of freedom and of impartial justice, or a more sympathetic treatment… '

↰ **SOURCE D:** *Written by Lord Lugard in* The Dual Mandate in British Tropical Africa, *1965.*

Take up the White Man's burden—
Send forth the best ye breed—
Go, bind your sons to exile
To serve your captives' need;
To wait in heavy harness,
On fluttered folk and wild—
Your new-caught, sullen peoples,
Half devil and half child.

↵ **SOURCE C:** *An extract from the poem* The White Man's burden *by British author Rudyard Kipling written in 1899. The poem was meant to encourage America to copy Britain and build an Empire.*

'India has become impoverished [poor] by their [Britain's] government. They take away our money from year to year. The most important jobs are reserved for themselves. We are kept in a state of slavery. They behave insolently [insultingly] towards us and disregard our feelings… '

↰ **SOURCE E:** *Written by Mohandas K. Gandhi in* Indian Home Rule, *1938.*

> 'When they first came they had the Bible and we had the land. We now have the Bible and they have our land.'

⌐ **SOURCE F:** *A popular African saying.*

> 'British brains and British money have transformed India. Thanks to improved sanitation, the development of transport and carefully thought-out relief work, famines have now virtually disapeared. To have conquered the menace of famine is a remarkable achievement for which India is wholly indebted to Britain.'

⌐ **SOURCE G:** *Written by Sir John A. R. Marriott in The English in India: A Problem of Politics, 1932.*

⌐ **SOURCE I:** *This is based on a cartoon that appeared in an Indian school textbook in 1986.*

Work

1 a Divide your page into two columns. Write a brief description of each source in the column in which you think it belongs. If you think it belongs in both, write a brief description overlapping both columns.

An Empire to be proud of?	An Empire to be ashamed of?

b Now, answer the question, 'Did Britain have an Empire to be proud of?' Make sure you mention the sources when explaining your answer.

⌐ **SOURCE H:** *The Scottish explorer David Livingstone once explained to a British audience: 'I go back to Africa to make an open path for commerce and Christianity'.*

_____ **MISSION ACCOMPLISHED?** _____

- Can you explain why some people believe that the British Empire was a bad thing?
- Do you know why others believe it benefited the world?
- Have you decided which you believe?

HOW TOLERANT WAS VICTORIAN BRITAIN?

The idea of slavery is a very old one. For thousands of years, men have captured 'weaker' people, treated them as their own private property and forced them to do their work. The Egyptians are believed, by many, to have used slaves to build the pyramids and the Romans forced slaves to fight in gladiator arenas for entertainment. But from around 1500 onwards, slavery turned into a highly profitable international business that forced millions of people to move to the other side of the world. So where did these slaves come from? Where were they moved to? And who became rich from this trade of human beings?

1: What was the slave trade?

MISSION OBJECTIVES

- To be able to define what a slave is.
- To know what was traded at each corner of the 'slave triangle'.
- To be able to explain how and why Britain was involved in the trade of human beings.

After two horrific months travelling across the Atlantic Ocean, the slaves were sold to farmers. The slave trader made a fortune while the slaves went to work on the huge **plantations** that grew sugar, cotton and tobacco. The slave trader then loaded his empty ship with these goods and headed back to Europe. When he returned home, the cotton-wearing, sugar-loving and tobacco-smoking people paid huge sums for his cargo. Having made big profits at each stage of the journey, the slave trader was ready to set sail all over again.

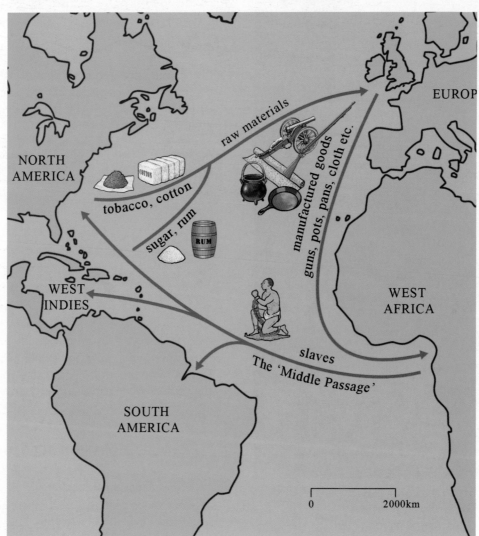

Slave traders, including many from Britain, loaded ships with goods that were cheap in Europe but highly priced in Africa – such as, guns, pots, kettles and necklaces.

The goods from Europe were unloaded and exchanged with African traders – not for valuables or money but for men, women and children.

↰ **SOURCE A:** *Slave traders at work: a painting of slave dealers on the coast of Africa.*

SOURCE B: *This was the official coat of arms for one English slave trader. He designed it himself and had these crests carved into most of his furniture in his London home!* ↱

WISE-UP Words

plantation
slave trader

Work ⌇⌇⌇⌇⌇.

1 Write a sentence or two to explain the following words: slave • slave trader • plantation.

2 a In your own words, explain how the slave trade was organised. Use a diagram to help you.

b Why was the slave trade so profitable?

c The slave trade is often referred to as 'triangular trade' or 'the slave triangle'. How do you think it got its name?

3 Look at Sources A and C. What similarities can you find between the scene in the painting and Source C?

4 Look closely at Source A. Can you spot the following:
i) A slave woman being burned with the mark of her owner?
ii) A slave being held down by two European men?
iii) A row of six slaves chained together by their necks?
iv) The African slave trader smoking?
v) The European slave trader with his log book?
vi) The slave ship?

'I saw many of my miserable countrymen chained together, some with their hands tied behind their backs. We were taken to a place near the coast and I asked the guide why we were here. He told me that I was to learn the ways of the white-faced people. He took a gun, some cloth and some metal in exchange for me. This made me cry bitterly. I was then taken to a ship where I saw my fellow captives moaning and crying.'

↰ **SOURCE C:** *This account was written by a slave who was taken to work in the West Indies. Years later, he was freed and taken to England.*

—————— **MISSION ACCOMPLISHED?** ——————

• Can you explain what the word 'slave' means?
• Do you know what was transported from Europe to Africa, from Africa to the Americas and from the Americas to Europe?
• Could you tell someone why people in Britain were involved?

The trade in slaves was driven by greed. Some Europeans realised they could become very rich by growing sugar, cotton and tobacco in the 'New World' and selling it back home. But they needed lots of people to work on the plantations growing these products – and they didn't want to pay them. Some Africans realised that they could make money by supplying slave labour to the Europeans. African men, women and children were usually captured by warriors from other tribes, kept in cages until a slave trader arrived, and then exchanged for goods. But how did they get to the plantations in the New World? Why were they treated the way they were? And how do we know about their horrific journeys?

2: On board the *Brookes*

MISSION OBJECTIVES

- To be able to explain how people ended up on slave ships.
- To evaluate sources in order to understand what conditions were like on board a slave ship.

One of the many ships that transported slaves across the Atlantic was called the *Brookes*, based in Liverpool. It made its owners a fortune by completing the journey around the 'slave triangle' a number of times. We know this because they kept detailed records of the journeys made, cargo carried and profits gained. After all, buying and selling human beings wasn't illegal, so slave traders treated it like any other professional business.

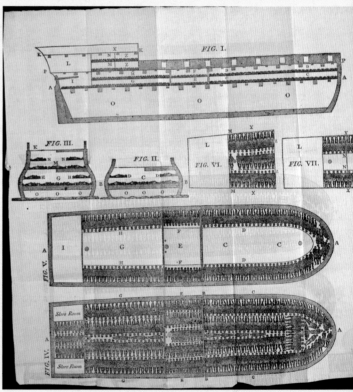

↰ SOURCE B: *A plan of the* Brookes. *No space was wasted.*

The owners of the *Brookes* decided that, if they crammed slaves into every square inch, they could carry over 400 slaves (see Source B). The distance between the decks was only 1.5m, so even if they weren't chained to the floor, the slaves were unable to stand up. Men were loaded into the bow (the front), children in the centre and women in the stern (back part of the ship).

↰ SOURCE A: *This eighteenth-century illustration shows slaves being loaded on board a ship for an Atlantic crossing.*

Life on board was horrific. Temperatures below deck reached 35°C and the lack of fresh air made seasickness and heatstroke very common. The only toilet was a bucket – but many were unable to reach it so they ended up lying in their own waste. The movement of the ship meant that, soon, everybody would be lying in it and, as a result, **dysentery**, a deadly form of diarrhoea, spread like wild fire among the slaves.

The journey lasted between 40 and 70 days and, from 1510 to 1833, over 10 million slaves were taken across the Atlantic in this way. It is estimated that some 2 million African people died making the crossing in ships like the *Brookes* during this time.

Despite the horrific death toll, slave traders actually wanted the slaves to be in good condition when they arrived at their destination. As they got nearer to the plantations, they were taken out to the top deck for air and exercise and given buckets of food to share. For those that survived the journey, the ordeal was still not over when they reached the shore. They then faced the prospect of being sold.

Work

1 a Why were so many slaves packed on board the ships?

b Why do you think the slaves were chained together for most of the voyage?

c Why do you think slave traders wanted slaves to be healthy and in good condition when they arrived? Does their treatment surprise you, then?

2 a Copy and complete the following table:

Source	What does it show?	Why is it useful to us today?

b Which source do you think is most useful to a historian? Give reasons for your explanation.

3 Many slave traders were very proud of the way they ran their businesses. They often invited observers on voyages to see the 'slave triangle' for themselves.

Imagine you are one such observer, invited onto the *Brookes* by a slave trader. Write a short letter to a friend, describing your journey and your feelings about the voyage.

4 a Each slave on the *Brookes* made an average of £22 profit for their dealer when sold. If the ship carried 410 slaves, how much profit would the slave trader make in total?

b Do the large profits justify the trade in human beings? Explain your answer carefully.

WISE-UP Words
dysentery

'The poor creatures, thus cramped for want of room, are likewise in irons, for the most part both hands and feet, and two together, which makes it difficult for them to turn or move, to rise or lie down, without hurting themselves.'

↳ SOURCE C: *Taken from the* Journal of a slave trader, *1788. Written by ex-slave trader, John Newton.*

'The floor was covered with blood and mucus. It looked like a slaughterhouse. After 15 minutes down there I had to leave. The heat and the stink made me nearly faint.'

↳ SOURCE D: *Written by a doctor after a visit to a slave ship.*

'Some died of dysentery, "the bloody flux". Others died of harsh treatment and poor food. Some with infectious diseases, such as smallpox, were thrown to the sharks. Others went mad and were clubbed to death. Some committed suicide by hanging themselves or jumping ship.'

↳ SOURCE E: *From* Black Peoples of the Americas *by Bea Stimpson, 2001.*

_____ **MISSION ACCOMPLISHED?** _____

• Could you tell someone how some Africans became slaves?

• Have you explained why the above sources are useful to us?

• Can you describe the conditions on board a slave ship?

Before any slaves were sold, they were cleaned up. They were washed down with water and given oil to rub into their skin to make them look shinier and healthier. Hot tar or rust was rubbed into any sores or ulcers picked up while crossing the Atlantic in order to disguise them. One ship's captain, whose slaves were suffering from terrible diarrhoea, instructed the doctor to push a short, thick piece of rope up the backside of each of them before the auction took place. So why did they want the slaves to look healthy? How did slaves change hands? And how did slave owners identify their new 'property'?

3: A slave sale

MISSION OBJECTIVES

- To be able to explain how traders prepared slaves in order to maximise their profits.
- To understand why some slaves were sold for a higher price than others.
- To be able to describe two separate ways in which slaves were sold.

There were two main ways to buy a slave: **auction** or **scramble**.

'Auction' – slaves were paraded in front of buyers and examined like cattle. They were then made to stand on an auction box and buyers would 'bid' for them. They were sold to the person who paid the most. Unhealthy, unsold slaves were left to die without food or water.

'Scramble' – the slave trader would set a fixed price for his slaves. At a given signal, usually a horn or a drumbeat, the buyers would rush into the cage and grab the slaves they liked the best. You can probably tell why it was called a scramble!

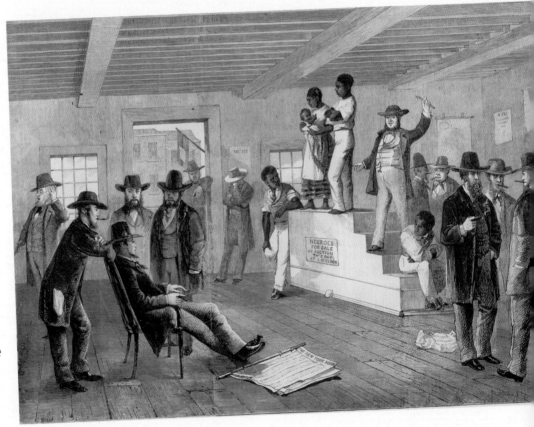

↰ SOURCE B: *A slave auction.*

'On a given signal, the buyers rush at once into the yard where the slaves are kept and make a choice of the one that they like best. The noise and clamour increases the worry of the terrified Africans. In this manner, relations and friends are separated, never to see each other again.'

↰ SOURCE A: *A description by Olaudah Equiano, who was sold at a 'scramble'.*

! FACT **Selling slaves**

In Jamaica in 1787, a slave called Jimmy fetched £330. He was a good carpenter 'in his prime'. At the same auction, a slave called Butler only cost 6d (2.5p). He was described as 'a very **indifferent** fellow with bad legs'.

and outlawed slavery. Plantation owners throughout the West Indies were terrified that the rebellion would spread and their crops would soon be in flames. White slave owners had argued that Africans were inferior to Europeans and that their natural position was to be following orders and doing simple, manual work. What had happened in Haiti had proved to many people that this argument was wrong – and so did the actions of some African people in Britain.

Although there was no law saying that slavery was illegal in Britain, there was no law saying it was legal either. Many slaves that had been brought to Britain from Africa or the West Indies went to court to claim their freedom. More and more judges, impressed by the slaves' arguments, allowed them to go free.

The incredible Equiano

One former slave, Olaudah Equiano, campaigned tirelessly to convince British people that the slave trade was wrong. He had been taken from his home in Africa to Barbados when he was just ten years old. He worked as a servant to a ship's captain, travelled widely, and learned to read and write while staying in England. He was then taken to North America and sold once more but, through incredible hard work and patience, he bought his freedom and moved back to Britain, where he got married and wrote his life story. This was widely read and turned many people in Britain against slavery. The fact that he was clearly intelligent and articulate made a nonsense out of the claims that Africans were inferior and only good for manual work.

↵ **SOURCE C:** *Equiano's tales of cruelty and inhumanity changed the attitudes of many people in Britain towards the slave trade.*

Reason 3: Wilberforce

Some people believe that it was the actions of religious Europeans that led to the outlawing of slavery. Granville Sharp helped many former slaves in their court cases against their old masters and did much to help bring the injustice of slavery to the British public's attention. In 1797, a group of 12 devout Christian men, led by William Wilberforce, formed a group to fight for abolition. Wilberforce was an MP and made many speeches against slavery in Parliament. Another member of the group, Thomas Clarkson, collected together evidence of the horrors of the middle passage and the treatment that the slaves faced. The campaigners, who all believed that slavery went against the teachings of Christ, then used this evidence to collect huge petitions from the public.

'The grand object of my parliamentary existence is the abolition of the slave trade. Before this great cause all others dwindle in my eyes. If it pleases God to honour me so far, may I be the instrument of stopping such a course of wickedness and cruelty as never before disgraced a Christian country.'

↳ **SOURCE D:** *From a speech by William Wilberforce in 1789.*

↵ **SOURCE E:** *200 000 of these seals were made and given away to try and convince people that slavery was evil and wrong.*

Work

1 Write a sentence explaining what the word 'abolish' means.

2 What do you think was the most important factor in causing the abolition of slavery? Write a paragraph explaining why you think it is more important than the other two factors.

3 Imagine you are a newspaper journalist in 1800. You work for one of the growing number of newspapers that are slowly turning against the idea of slavery. Your editor has asked you to compile a 'news exclusive' called 'SLAVERY – THE REAL STORY'.
- Write one article about the slave trade itself – how does the 'slave triangle' operate?
- Write one about conditions on board a slave ship – why do so many slaves die?
- Write another about the sale of slaves and the work on the plantations – what work did slaves do and why were they punished so severely?
- Also write about the campaign to end slavery – who are the key figures?
- Include appropriate pictures and quotes.

4 Do you think Victorian Britain was a tolerant place? Explain your answer carefully.

MISSION ACCOMPLISHED?

- Can you tell someone how many years it has been since slavery was made illegal in Britain?
- Have you decided what caused the change in attitudes towards slavery in Britain?

WHO RULES?

On the 10 April 1848, a meeting was planned at Kennington Common, South London. Half a million people were expected to attend… and they all wanted change. In particular, they demanded big changes to the way in which the country was ruled. After the meeting, the people were going to march through London to Parliament and hand in a petition that reportedly contained 6 million signatures, outlining the changes they wanted to happen. Feargus O'Connor, a man who was due to speak at the meeting, had even published new plans for running the country… with him as the new president!

1: How close was a British revolution?

MISSION OBJECTIVES

- To understand how people fought for their rights between 1750 and 1900.
- To be able to judge how successful they were.

As you might have expected, the government saw the massive meeting of angry people at Kennington Common as a threat. They thought it might have been the start of a revolution similar to those that had taken place in other countries. As a precaution, Queen Victoria was moved out of London to the safety of the Isle of Wight, 1.5 million new policemen were signed up and 100 000 heavily armed soldiers were brought in to protect the city. The old war hero, the Duke of Wellington, was even put in charge of London's defences and took over all the railways and telegraph services.

So what was it about the way the country was governed that had made these people so angry? What exactly were the changes that the protestors wanted? And were their demands eventually met?

SOURCE A: *The Kennington Common Rally, April 1848.*

FACT The Luddites

Some workers were upset that new factory machinery could do the work that maybe ten men used to do. These men formed gangs and went around smashing up the new machinery. In 1811, the machine-smashers or Luddites, as they became known, destroyed machines in the Midlands, Yorkshire and Lancashire. They were led by a man called Ned Ludd, who lived secretly in Sherwood Forest, Nottingham – but no one ever found him (perhaps he never really existed?). The gangs caused thousands of pounds worth of damage – and the government took strict action. Machine-smashing became a crime punishable by death.

FACT The Swingers

In 1830, the machine-smashers reappeared. This time, workers in the countryside attacked farm machinery because farmers began to use machines to do the work that men used to do. Fields were set on fire, farmhouses were burned down and barns smashed up. Farmers received threatening letters, often signed by 'Captain Swing', the leader of the rioters (it is unlikely he existed any more than Ned Ludd did!). Again, the government took tough action. Nineteen people were hanged, 644 were put in prison and 481 were transported to Australia. Despite the riots, farmers continued to use the new machinery and many farm workers left the countryside to look for work in the towns and cities.

FACT The Peterloo Massacre

For many hundreds of years, only a small number of men (rich ones) had been allowed to vote in elections. Many ordinary people, who couldn't vote, felt this was unfair. They thought that MPs would listen more closely to their complaints about their lives if they were voters. In August 1819, a huge, non-violent meeting was held in St Peter's Field, Manchester. Thousands of men, women and children attended carrying banners demanding 'Votes for All'. However, things soon got out of hand. The government sent in soldiers to arrest the speakers and break up the crowd. But the sword-waving soldiers managed to kill 11 people and injure 400 more. The youngest victim was a baby, William Fildes, who was knocked out of his mother's arms and trampled to death by horses.

SOURCE B: *People soon called the massacre 'Peterloo', a sarcastic reference to the famous Battle of Waterloo, when British soldiers defeated the French in 1815.* ↱

The fight for rights

One of the hottest topics in Britain in the 1800s was the issue of 'who rules?' Increasing numbers of ordinary people wanted to choose their leaders by voting for them in elections. They felt that having the 'right to vote' would mean that the politicians who ran the government might attack some of the problems in their lives. This system of choosing leaders through voting is known as 'democracy'.

Democracy in the early 1800s

Many people in the early 1800s felt that the system of establishing who ruled the country was unfair – what do you think? Look carefully at Source C, which outlines how Britain's voting system worked in the early 1800s.

Election time

The election described in Source D, typical of one in the early 1800s, was a poor way to find people to run the country. Clearly there were problems with Britain's democratic system. Not many people could vote for a start (1 in 40) and their vote wasn't even secret, so people could be bribed to vote by those who wanted to become MPs. Also, some places (called 'rotten boroughs') only had a couple of voters (Appleby in Cumbria had one voter) yet still sent an MP to parliament to help run Britain. And some places like Birmingham, Liverpool and Manchester (which were now large towns) didn't even have their own MPs.

❚❚ PAUSE for Thought

What do you think is meant by the word 'democracy'? Discuss it as a class or write down your own definitions of the word.

ELECTION RULES, 1830

- No man under 21 can vote... and no women at all!

- Only men who own property worth 40 shillings per year (if they were to rent it out) can vote.

- Voting is not secret... you have to announce who you're voting for.

- Each man standing for election is called a **candidate**. The candidate with most votes becomes the Member of Parliament (**MP**) for that area... and you're not paid to do the job.

- As an MP, you will probably belong to one of the two main political parties – the **Whigs** or the **Tories**. The Whigs feel that some changes are needed to the voting system (and Britain in general), whilst the Tories don't want any changes at all.

- The political party which has the most MPs forms the government and its leader becomes Prime Minister (PM). The government makes the laws. The king or queen doesn't interfere too much so running Britain is left up to the PM and his MPs.

↰ SOURCE C: *Democracy in the 1800s.*

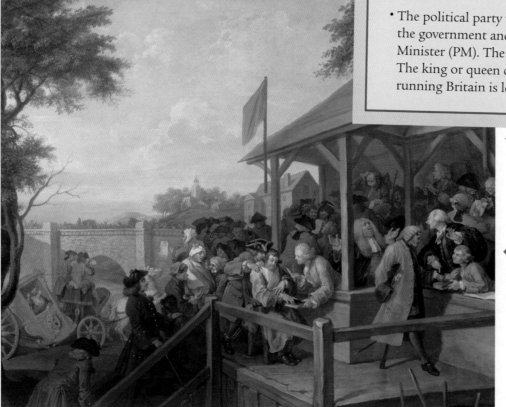

↵ SOURCE D: The Polling *by William Hogarth, 1755. Can you see:*
i) The rich men being brought in on their carriages to vote?
ii) One of the voters (underneath the blue flag) being told how to vote?
iii) Two thugs dragging a sick man to the election so he can vote?

Change at last

By 1832, some MPs were beginning to fear that the revolution was near. Hundreds of thousands of people were demonstrating about the voting system all over Britain. They saw change – or '**reform**' as it was known – as their great hope for a better life. Politicians worried that a demonstration might turn into a riot (as they often did) and that the rioters might become strong enough to take over the country by force, removing those currently in power. These MPs realised that change was essential and introduced a new system of voting (see Source E).

How great was the Great Reform Act?

The changes made in 1832 are often called the 'Great Reform Act' by historians. But was it so great? Still only one in five men could vote... and no women! You still had to own property to vote and there were still some rotten boroughs. And voting still wasn't secret – which led to the problems encountered in Source F.

The 'Great' Reform Act was a huge disappointment for many ordinary working men. They wanted the vote but still didn't get it. Yes, the changes were a move in the right direction, but still four out of five men had no rights over their country. In 1836, a new campaign group was formed. Most members of this group simply wanted more change – but others wanted to take over the country and change it by force.

The government soon saw these men as a massive threat – they were known as the Chartists.

The Reform Act, 1832
- More people were allowed to vote – increase in voters from 450 000 to 800 000.
- Some big towns like Manchester and Birmingham were given MPs for the first time.
- Some of the old 'rotten boroughs' were removed.

⤴ **SOURCE E:** *The main points of the new voting system.*

'Everybody was told that if they voted against Colonel Anson they would be in trouble, if they voted for him they were greeted with loud cheers. If they voted for Sir Goodricke they were hissed, booed and spat on. One voter had a load of horse dung thrown all over him and dead birds were thrown at another.'

⤴ **SOURCE F:** *An account of an election in Wolverhampton in 1835.*

The Chartists – reformers or revolutionaries?

In 1838, a meeting was held in Birmingham to draw up a list of desirable changes to the voting system in Britain. Ordinary working people attended the meeting – printers, shopkeepers, tailors, carpenters, shoemakers, newsagents and factory workers. The meeting agreed on six demands and the list was called the People's Charter. Those who agreed with the 'Charter' became known as Chartists.

↵ **SOURCE G:** *This is what the Chartists wanted. They discussed the possibility of including 'votes for women' but decided this was a step too far!*

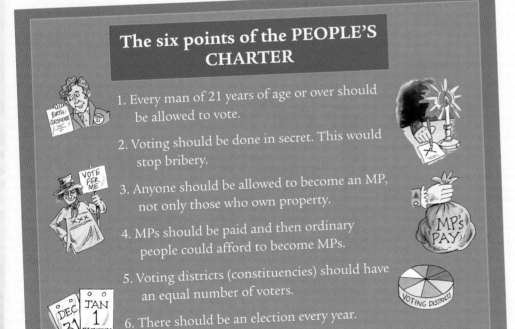

The six points of the PEOPLE'S CHARTER

1. Every man of 21 years of age or over should be allowed to vote.

2. Voting should be done in secret. This would stop bribery.

3. Anyone should be allowed to become an MP, not only those who own property.

4. MPs should be paid and then ordinary people could afford to become MPs.

5. Voting districts (constituencies) should have an equal number of voters.

6. There should be an election every year.

All Chartists wanted change. They saw that many rich people in Britain were getting even richer, but most workers remained poor... and lived in horrible conditions. They wanted the government to help them, but believed they didn't care! Some workers even lost their jobs because new machinery replaced them. They felt that very little was done to help them because there was no one to speak up for them. The Charter would be their attempt to make the voting system fairer – and open to all (except women – maybe later!). If working men had the vote, they could elect MPs who promised to look after them!

For the Chartists, persuading Parliament to adopt their ideas was the difficult part. They held huge rallies in big cities such as Birmingham, Liverpool and Leeds, hoping to attract support and show the government that a huge number of people agreed with them. Then, in 1839, they drew up a petition, signed by over 1 million people (it was three miles long!) who supported the Chartists' ideas. The petition was sent to Parliament so that MPs could see how many people wanted the changes.

Parliament ignored the petition when it arrived at their door. So another petition was organised, this time containing 3 million signatures. Yet again, Parliament ignored it. Some Chartist leaders started to get angry at Parliament's refusal to listen. Some talked about revolution, taking the country over and forcing the changes. Others continued to encourage the old-fashioned, peaceful methods. Read Sources H and I carefully. Try to work out which one of the leaders wants to use force and which one wants to remain peaceful.

> 'Let us, friends, seek to join together the honest, moral, hard-working and intelligent members of society. Let us find out about our rights from books. Let us collect information about our lives, our wages and our conditions. Then let us publish our views. Then MPs will agree there must be change, without having to use violence or arrest.'

↳ **SOURCE H:** *From a speech by William Lovett, one of the Chartist leaders.*

> 'I do not want to use force, but if we do not succeed we must use violence. It is better to die free men than live as slaves. Violence is the right thing to do if it wins us our freedom.'

↳ **SOURCE I:** *From a speech made by Feargus O'Connor, another Chartist leader.*

One more try

In 1848, a third petition was organised. This one had over 6 million signatures! The Chartists planned a huge meeting of over half a million people on Kennington Common, South London, before marching to Parliament with their demands.

The government was worried – was this the start of a revolution? Plans were drawn up to defend London and Queen Victoria was moved to safety. But the meeting was a huge flop. It rained heavily and around only 20 000 Chartists turned up (see Source A). That's right, a possible revolution failed because of bad weather!

The petition turned out to be a bit of a flop too. When Parliament inspected it, it was found to contain just over 2 million names – and many of them were fakes. Queen Victoria herself was supposed to have signed it ten times, as well as 'April First', 'Cheeks the Marine', 'No Cheese', 'Pug Nose', 'The Duke of Wellington' (nine times), 'Long Nose' and 'Mr Punch'! After their failure in 1848, little was heard of the Chartists again. They had failed... or had they?

SOURCE J: *A cartoon from* Punch *magazine showing the meeting on Kennington Common. The cartoonist has shown the Duke of Wellington nine times! Do you think the cartoonist is making fun of the petition or not?* ↳

A success story

The Chartists were the first organised national protest movement. They drew attention to the problems and frustrations of the working-class people and showed that there were national issues that the government must pay attention to. In fact, of their six original demands, all but one (Point 6) later became law!

For a few brief days in the spring of 1848, the government had feared the Chartists. How close Britain came to a revolution is open for discussion but the Chartists certainly showed that working people were powerful (and potentially threatening) if they joined together… and that politicians should listen to them a bit more in the future!

Power to the people

The changes to the way people voted continued after the Chartist movement. In 1867, the Second Reform Act gave the vote to every man who owned a house (which was one in three men) and, in 1884, the Third Reform Act gave even more working people the vote. Consequently, the number of voters rose from about 3 million to approximately 5 million, meaning two out of three men could now vote. In 1872, the Ballot Act said that people could vote by putting their ballot paper in a ballot box. This stopped people bribing and bullying voters into voting for them. And many more changes followed (see Source K). In fact, electoral reform is known as a continuing process.

WISE-UP Words

candidate MP
reform Tories Whigs

Electoral reforms

1832 First Reform Act.

1858 Any man over 21 allowed to become an MP, despite whether they owned property or not.

1867 Second Reform Act (one man in a three could now vote).

1872 Ballot Act (voting now done in secret).

1884 Third Reform Act (two out of every three men could now vote).

1885 Voting districts (constituencies) to have equal number of voters.

1911 MPs paid.

1918 All men over 18 and women over 30 could vote.

1928 Vote for everyone over 21.

1969 Vote for everyone over 18.

↖ SOURCE K: *Electoral reforms.*

— MISSION ACCOMPLISHED? —

- Can you explain what is meant by the term 'electoral reform' and give at least five examples?

Work

1 a What did Luddites and Swing Rioters have in common?

  b In what ways were they different?

2 Why do you think they both failed?

3 Why were Ned Ludd and Captain Swing never caught?

4 Explain what is happening in Source D. Refer to as many details in the painting as possible.

5 a Using pages 138 and 139, make a list of things that were either wrong or unfair about the voting system before 1832.

  b Can you think of any new voting rules that could be introduced to stop some of the problems you've noted in your answer to a?

6 a Who were the Chartists?

  b List their six demands.

  c Pick two that you think were most important to the workers. Give reasons for your choices.

  d Which of the six demands is not in force today?

  e Can you think why this has never been made a law?

7 Look at Sources H and I.

  a Rewrite each source in your own words.

  b Write a sentence to explain these two words:

    reformer • revolutionary.

  c In your opinion, who was the reformer and who was the revolutionary? Give reasons for your decision.

8 Write an essay that answers the question, 'Were the Chartists a success or not?' Organise your essay into short paragraphs:
- What changes did the Chartists want?
- Why did working people join them?
- How did they try to get change?
- What had they achieved by 1850?
- Were they a long-term success, rather than a short-term one?

How did Britain change between 1750 and 1900?

────────────── MISSION OBJECTIVES ──────────────

- To understand how Britain changed between 1750 and 1900 in key areas such as, population, transport, politics, leisure and health, and medicine.

This book covers the years 1750 to 1900. During this time, some amazing and lasting changes took place. It was a period in British history when great industrial towns and cities appeared, full of people linked together by roads, canals and trains that ran through the countryside. By 1900, most people were better fed, clothed, healthier and more educated than anyone could have imagined in 1750. Shops contained goods from all over the world, brought to Britain in huge steamships, which stood in newly built docks.

Today's Britain is full of reminders from this period. If you look around any town or city, you will see bridges, railways, stations, pubs, statues, libraries, churches, town halls and even school buildings that were designed and built between 1750 and 1900. Some of you may even live in houses built during this time. Much of what we take for granted today – light bulbs, cameras, motor cars, telephones, post boxes, even the basic rules of sports like rugby, cricket and football – came from the period covered in this book.

Read this section carefully. It doesn't feature all the changes, discoveries and inventions that took place between 1750 and 1900, but it tries to pick out some of the most important and interesting ones.

Travel

1750: Very slow. London to Edinburgh took two weeks by road… and the roads were terrible!

1900: Much faster. London to Edinburgh, took nine hours by train. The roads were better… and the motor car had been invented.

Population

1750: 7 million
80% lived in the countryside.

1900: 37 million
80% lived in towns and cities.

Leisure time

1750: Working people had few holidays. Blood sports very popular.

1900: Working people enjoyed shorter working hours and, therefore, more leisure time. Sports became more organised.

Law and order

1750: No police force and the death penalty for lots of crimes. Transportation also common.

1900: A professional police force and the death penalty only for very serious crimes. Prisons reformed and transportation stopped.

Politics

1750: Only 5% of the population could vote in elections. No women could vote.

1900: Now most men could vote but still no women could vote.

Health and medicine

1750: People didn't know that germs caused disease. If a person reached the age of one, they might expect to live to the age of 40. Operations were very dangerous.

1900: Knowledge that germs caused disease. Inventions such as, vaccinations, antiseptic and anaesthetics meant that if you reached the age of one, you might expect to live to the age of 55.

Joe Average
Born 1750
Died 1790
Age 40

John Average
Born 1890
Died 1945
Age 55

Work

1750: The farming industry is the largest employer, particularly for wool and food production. Manufacturing took place on a small scale, often in people's homes. Wind, horse, water and hand power used.

1900: Industry is dominated by coal, iron, steel and cloth. Steam-powered factories are a common sight.

The British Empire

1750:

1900:

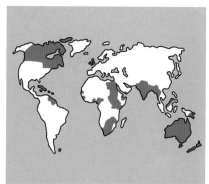

Education

1750: In England, most children did not go to school and few could read or write. In Scotland there were lots of schools and most people were literate. School was not compulsory.

1900: School compulsory for all 5–12 year olds. Newspapers and book publishing were expanding.

Food

1750: Bread, cheese, meat and vegetables were the main foods. All meals were home-made.

1900: Frozen meat and fish, foreign fruit, tinned and packet food introduced.

✚ Hungry for **MORE**

One of the world's most famous newspapers, *The Times*, first appeared on sale in 1785. In small groups, produce your own version of *The Times* but write it to cover the whole period of 1750–1900. Write articles for each of the following headlines:

- Living and working
- The fight for rights
- Crime and punishment
- Sports pages
- Designers, inventors and engineers.
- Health news
- Women's page
- The Empire
- Getting around

Work

1 a Copy one of the sentences below that best describes Britain in 1900:

- Britain had changed completely between 1750 and 1900.
- Britain had changed a lot by 1900 but some things had not changed.
- Britain had not changed at all between 1750 and 1900.

2 a Divide a page, or a sheet of paper, into three: one-third for 1750, one-third for 1900 and one-third for today. Using the headings from the ten boxes on these pages, compare life in Britain during 1750, 1900 and today. You can use drawings and/or writing, and you may have to do some extra research for some of the figures (for example, for population figures of today).

3 Why not find out more about some of the products and inventions mentioned on this double page? Prepare fact-files on some (or all) of them.

↳ SOURCE A: *Coca-Cola was one of the many now familiar products and inventions that appeared between 1750 and 1900. Others include Christmas cards (1842), motor cars (1863), Levi jeans (1873), the telephone (1876), bras (1889), zips (1891) and breakfast cereals (1893 – Shredded Wheat). Coca-Cola (1886) was invented by a chemist who was looking for a headache cure. It was named after its original ingredients – coca leaves (also used to make cocaine!) and kola nuts.*

___MISSION ACCOMPLISHED?___

- Can you pick out your top five changes in Britain between 1750 and 1900?

Have you been learning? 3

TASK 1 Homophones

A homophone is a word that sounds the same as another word but has a different meaning and spelling. For example, a 'sale' in the shops and a 'sail' on a ship. The words sound the same but they are not spelled the same.

a Copy the sentences below, choosing the correct words from the choices in brackets:

   i) In 1750, most goods were (scent/sent) from one (plaice/place) to another by (road/rowed). This took a long (time/thyme). (By/Buy) 1900, the railways had sped up the process and become the (main/mane) method of transporting goods around Britain.

   ii) (There/Their) were (sum/some) (foul/fowl) factory towns in Victorian Britain. Litter and human (waist/waste) were just (throne/thrown) into the streets and most toilets were little more than a (whole/hole) in the ground.

   iii) (They're/There/Their) was (no/know) proper police force before 1829. Then Robert Peel set up Britain's first Metropolitan Police Force in London (in/inn) response (to/two) the growing crime rate. It was a (great/grate) success and the 'boys in (blew/blue)' have (bean/been) patrolling (hour/our) streets ever since.

b Try making up your own sentences that are full of homophones. Base them on your knowledge and understanding of your history lesson.

TASK 2 Analysing a source

A poster advertising a slave auction. The word 'griffe' means mixed race.

SLAVES FOR SALE
BY DOVE, FREEMAN & CO.
G T DOVE, Auctioneer

WILL BE SOLD AT AUCTION ON
THURSDAY 6 FEBRUARY
AT 1 O'CLOCK AT RIVER HALLS

1   JAMES, 13 years of age, good waiter; smart.
2   CATHERINE, 24 years of age, excellent house servant; well mannered; fully guaranteed.
3   ANNE, 19 years of age, house servant with fine temper.
4   JOHN, 17 years of age, a griffe, fine waiter and good servant, in his prime.
5   WILLIAM, 41 years of age, a field hand, fully guaranteed.
6   MARY, 24 years of age, skills in washing and ironing; intelligent.
7   HENRY, 20 years of age, field hand with a good character.
8   RICHARD, 17 years of age, a griffe man, waiter and servant; indifferent with a bad arm.
9   EMILY, 16 years of age, fine house girl; speaks French and English.
10 ANNE, 13 years of age, good house girl; fine temper.
11 AGNES, 22 years of age, excellent washer, ironer and cook. Superior nurse, fully guaranteed.
12 EDWARD, 20 years of age, field hand with an excellent character. Also excellent barber and trustworthy house servant.

TERMS CASH Sales by G T DOVE

Read the poster above carefully.
a Describe what a 'slave auction' was.
b What other way could slaves be sold?
c Which slaves do you think fetched the highest price at this auction? Give reasons for your answer.
d Which slaves (or slave) do you think were sold for the cheapest price? Give reasons for your answer.
e This is what a priest told slaves who were about to be auctioned in 1806: 'Your bodies, you know, are not your own; they are at the disposal of those you belong to.' What do you think the priest meant?

TASK 3 Note making

Note making is an important skill. To do it successfully, you must pick out any key words in each sentence. The key words are the ones that are vital to the meaning of the sentence. Without these words, the sentence makes no sense.

For example: 'Arthur Wharton, who lived from 1865 to 1930, was the world's first professional black footballer. He played professional cricket too!'

The key words are: Arthur Wharton; 1865 to 1930; world's first professional black footballer; cricket.

a Now write down the key words in the following sentences. The key words are your notes.

- Between 1750 and 1840, there were over 700 full-scale riots in Britain.

- Some of the riots were started by men who were unhappy that only a small number of rich men were allowed to vote in elections.

- As the riots got more and more violent, Parliament allowed a few more to vote. However, by 1832, Parliament allowed only around one in five men to vote… and no women.

- One of the most famous groups to insist on gaining the right to vote was the Chartists. They collected millions of signatures on a petition that demanded changes to the voting system.

- They also organised a huge meeting in London in 1848, which worried the government so much that they sent Queen Victoria to the Isle of Wight! However, not many went to the meeting because it rained.

- Eventually, over several years, Parliament gave more and more people the vote. By 1884, two out of every three British men held the right to vote.

- However, all women didn't have the right to vote until 1928.

b Why not make notes on other topics or parts of your work notes?

TASK 4 Victorian celebrities

a Draw this puzzle in your book and fill in the answers to the clue:

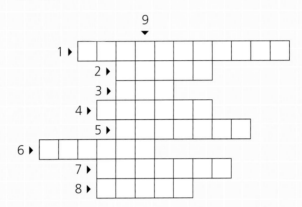

Clue 1: An MP who pushed to end slavery.

Clue 2: He set up the NSPCC.

Clue 3: A prison reformer… on a £5 note.

Clue 4: The smallpox saviour.

Clue 5: Louis the 'germ hero'.

Clue 6: An antiseptic superstar.

Clue 7: The chocolate champion.

Clue 8: He set up the Salvation Army.

b Now read '9 down' in the puzzle and write a sentence or two about this famous man.

TASK 5 Firsts

There are two parts to this task.

a Work through the seven 'firsts' featured below, finding out the date of each one.

b Then put the 'firsts' in chronological order.

i) First telephone

ii) First Sainsbury's store

iii) The world's first railway locomotive, built by Richard Trevithick

iv) First Cricket Test Match between England and Australia

v) First Wimbledon Tennis Tournament

vi) World's first official police force goes into action

vii) World's first football league is won.

Glossary

Abolished Brought to an end. For example, the slave trade.

Aborigines People who lived in Australia and Tasmania before the British arrived.

Alcoholic Someone who is addicted to alcohol.

Ammunition Objects, such as bullets, that are fired from guns.

Amputate To cut off a part of the body, such as a leg or arm.

Anaesthetic A substance that stops you feeling pain.

Antiseptic A chemical that prevents infection by killing germs.

Apprentice house Accommodation built next to factories, where pauper apprentices lived.

Aqueduct A bridge that carries a canal over an obstacle (such as a river).

Arthritis Painful swelling of the joints and muscles.

Artillery Soldiers who fight with firearms.

Auction A public sale in which goods are sold to the person who offers the highest price.

Back-to-back housing Rows of houses, built very close together without room for a garden.

Bearer A mining job: children who carried coal-sacks around the pit.

'Black gold' The name given to coal by many mine owners, due to the large amount of money they made from it.

Black lung A nickname for a miner's illness that resulted in coughing fits and shortness of breath.

Blood sports Watching and betting on fighting animals. The craze began to die out in the 1850s.

Boards of Health Groups set up in some towns to investigate how the disease cholera spread and how it could be prevented.

Boers Descendants of Dutch settlers living in South Africa.

Bow Street Runners The forerunners of the police force – a group of men who were paid to capture as many criminals as possible.

Branded Permanently marked by burning skin with a hot metal instrument. Used to show who owned slaves.

Broadsides All the guns along one side of a warship – often all fired at the same time.

Camber Curved surface (of a road).

Canal A long, narrow, man-made channel of water.

Canal locks Gated boxes that keep the water level when a canal passes over a hill.

'Canal mania' A time between 1761 and about 1830 when many canals were built all over Britain.

Capital crimes Crimes that carry the death penalty.

Carding Combing or untangling wool before spinning.

Cast iron Iron that has been heated into a liquid and placed in a mould to make a shape.

Census Official count of the population, done every ten years in Britain.

Chain shot A type of ammunition, used to destroy sails and rigging.

Chloroform A strong smelling liquid that was used as an anaesthetic.

Cholera A disease caused by infected food or water. Victims suffer from diarrhoea, vomiting and can die.

Clerk A person whose job is to keep records or accounts in an office, bank or court.

Clothier A person who buys and sells wool/cloth.

Coalface The area where coal is dug out of the ground.

Coining Making fake coins or shaving bits of metal away from the edges of coins in order to make other ones with the bits.

Coke Coal that has been heated to remove the sulphur. Used to make cast iron.

Colonies Areas of land in the world ruled by a country – in this case, Britain.

Commuting Travelling to work.

Contradicted Went against; disagreed with.

Constable An unpaid person, who tried to keep law and order in his town for a period of one year.

Convert Change, for example, one's religion.

Costermonger A street trader.

Coup d'état The sudden and forcible takeover of the government of a country by other people from that country – for example, when Napoleon seized power of France in 1799.

Dame school A basic school run by women, often in the front room of their house. Students paid a few pennies to attend.

Destitute Poverty-stricken; having nothing.

Domestic system The system where people worked in their homes or small workshops rather than in factories.

Dominant species The most common species (type of animal) in an area, or the species that has the greatest access to resources, such as food.

Drawer A mining job: children who pushed and pulled loaded coal wagons in the pit.

Dysentery A deadly form of diarrhoea.

Empire A collection of colonies all ruled by one 'mother country'.

Enclosure When farmers bought strips of land from their neighbours, creating a large farm area, and surrounded their land with hedges and fences.

Entrepreneur A business person who takes risks, often with their own money, in order to make a profit.

Epidemic Rapid spread of a disease.

Ether A colourless liquid that was used as an anaesthetic.

Evolved Changed over time to suit the environment in which something lives, such as the climate or the type of food available.

Factory system The system where people worked in factories to produce goods in large numbers where they used to be produced in people's homes or in small workshops. Replaced the domestic system.

Fallow Land not being used.

Flying shuttle A 1733 invention in the cloth industry, this machine sped up weaving.

Four-course rotation Growing four different crops, over four years, in four different fields.

Gallows A wooden frame used for hanging criminals.

Grape shot A type of ammunition – canvas bags full of lumps of metal that would spread out when fired.

Greenwich Mean Time The name given to British time when it was standardised in 1852 – the local time in Greenwich (London) began to be used for the whole country.

Hops Plants used for brewing beer.

Immigration Coming to a foreign country in order to settle there.

Imported Brought in from another country, usually to be sold.

Incentive Something that encourages an effort or action; it motivates people to do something.

Independence Existing separately from other people or things. An independent nation has no help from another country.

Indifferent Not bothered, showing no interest. Poor quality.

Industrial Revolution A complete change in the way things were made. A time when factories replaced farming as the main form of business in Britain. Sometimes used to describe the changes in population, transport, cities and so on in the period between 1750 and 1900.

Industry The work and methods involved in making things in factories.

Infantry Foot soldiers.

Iron ore Dug from the ground; the raw material used to make iron.

Ironworks A factory that makes things from iron.

Labour saving Making life easier by saving us time and effort.

Laissez-faire A French word meaning 'leave alone'.

Lashed Whipped.

Literacy Ability to read and write.

Locomotive An engine used to pull trucks or passenger carriages along a track.

Logbook An official record of the school.

Loom A machine for weaving cloth.

Lunar Society A group of men, who discussed how to use new developments in science to improve people's lives.

Magazine Stock of ammunition.

Manufacture Make goods in a factory.

Marines Soldiers, mainly serving at sea.

Maternity Relating to or involving pregnant women and birth.

Mechanised If work is mechanised, machines are installed to do it.

Melodramas Musical plays with very dramatic plots and exaggerated emotions.

Miasma 'Bad air', believed by many to be the cause of diseases such as cholera.

Midwives Nurses trained to help women at the birth of a baby.

Miners Workers who dig coal out of the ground.

Modus operandi Originally a Latin phrase, meaning 'modes of operation', used to describe a criminal's methods and style of committing crimes.

Morse code A system of dots and dashes invented in 1844, which was used for sending telegraphs.

Music halls Venues putting on a wide variety of entertainment acts. Cheaper to visit than theatres.

Muzzle A cover or strap that covers up the nose and mouth.

Navvies Workers employed to build roads, railways, canals or buildings.

Nonconformist A person who had their own style of worship, rather than following the rules and practices of the Church of England.

Nystagmus An eye illness caused by many years of straining to see in poor light.

Observation Watching something carefully and recording your findings.

Okra A tropical plant with long green edible pods.

Overseer A man in charge of the factory workers on a day-to-day basis, like a manager.

Pardoned Officially released from punishment for a crime.

Pasteurisation Heating of food and drink, for example, milk, to kill germs.

Pauper Someone who is extremely poor.

Pauper apprentices An orphan, who worked in a factory in return for food and a bed.

Philanthropist Someone who freely gives help or money to people in need.

Piracy Being a pirate, a person who robs people at sea.

Plantation A huge farm that grows cotton, sugar, tobacco, and so on. A plantation owner normally used slaves to do the work.

'Pleads her belly' A plea by a woman on trial for a crime. Pleading her belly meant she was claiming to be pregnant and asking to be found not guilty of the crime.

Population The number of people in a particular place at a particular time.

Powder monkeys Boys working on ships, who fetched gunpowder from the magazine and took it to the guns.

Prostitute A person, usually a woman, who has sex with men in exchange for money.

Ragged school A charity school, which was free to attend for very poor children.

Raking Firing along the length of something, for example, a line of ships.

Raw materials Natural substances, such as coal, iron ore, gold, oil and so on.

Reformer A person who wants things (like living or working conditions) to change for the better.

Refrigeration A way of keeping something very cold in order to preserve it.

Revolt A violent attempt by a group of people to change the people who rule them.

Revolution The overthrow of one ruler or government and its replacement with another.

Rheumatism Painful stiffness in the joints and muscles.

Round shot A type of ammunition – solid metal balls 15cm in diameter.

Rural Relating to the countryside.

Ruts Deep holes in roads.

Scramble A method of buying slaves. A price is agreed before the buyers rush into a cage to grab the best slave they can.

Selective breeding Deliberately controlling the breeding of animals, for example, to breed larger animals.

Sepsis Poisoning or infection.

Sharpshooters Gunmen who stayed on their own ships and shot at the enemy from a distance.

Shifts Set working hours, for example, in factories.

Slave trader A person who buys and sells slaves.

Smallpox A disease that causes a fever and a rash. Can cause death.

Smelt Produce a metal (for example, iron) from its ore.

Social pyramid A name given to the structure of society. The richest people are at the very top of the pyramid, with the working class at the very bottom.

Specialisation A method of farming used by some areas after 1750, when farmers concentrated on (specialised in) growing certain crops.

Spinning jenny A 1764 invention in the cloth industry, this machine made the production of thread quicker by spinning more threads at the same time.

Steam engine An engine that uses steam as a means of power.

Sterilised A sterilised object is free from any germs.

Strip farming The old method of farming, also known as the 'open field system', in which people farmed small strips of land dotted all over their village. It was largely replaced by enclosure after 1750.

Suburbs Areas of a town or city that are away from the centre.

'Sun and planets' gear system A system used to turn the wheel in a steam engine.

Surplus An amount left over.

Telegraph An 1844 invention that was used to send messages via electrical pulses.

Terraces Rows of houses.

Theory of evolution A scientific principle first published by Charles Darwin in 1859 – the idea that all living things had gradually evolved (developed) over millions of years, rather than being created by God.

Toll An amount of money charged for using a stretch of road or a bridge.

Toll keeper A person who collected money (tolls) so that travellers could use a turnpike road.

Transportation A punishment. Guilty criminals could be sent to a far away land for a period of five, seven or fourteen years.

Trapper A mining job: children who opened and closed trapdoors in the pit.

Turnpike road A stretch of road with gates at the end where tolls were collected by toll keepers.

Turnpike trust A group of businessmen, who improved and maintained a stretch of road and charged people to use it.

Tutor A teacher.

Vaccination The process of giving someone a vaccine (a substance made from the germs that cause a disease), usually by injection, which protects them against disease by making them immune to it.

Viaduct A long, high bridge that carries a road or railway over an obstacle (such as a valley or river).

Watchman A paid volunteer who tried to catch criminals.

Wrought iron Iron that has been heated up and hammered into shape. More flexible than cast iron.

Yam A vegetable that grows in hot regions. Also called a sweet potato.

Yarn Thread used for knitting or making cloth.

Index